Editor
Kim Fields

Managing Editor
Mara Ellen Guckian

Illustrator
Mark Mason

Cover Artist
Kevin Barnes

Editor in Chief
Ina Massler Levin, M.A.

Creative Director
Karen J. Goldfluss, M.S. Ed.

Art Coordinator
Renée Christine Yates

Imaging
James Edward Grace
Craig Gunnell

Publisher

Mary D. Smith, M.S. Ed.

W9-BGW-398

Includes Standards & Benchmarks

Grades 3 - 5

GOING GREEN

RESPOND · REFUSE · REDUCE · REUSE · RECYCLE · RESEARCH

Author

Tracie Heskett, M.Ed.

Teacher Created Resources, Inc.
6421 Industry Way
Westminster, CA 92683
www.teachercreated.com

ISBN: 978-1-4206-2547-9

© 2010 Teacher Created Resources, Inc.
Made in U.S.A.

Teacher Created Resources

Table of Contents

Introduction

Get ready for *Going Green.* This book will help encourage your students to take care of the environment by adapting the way they live and do things—beginning in the classroom. The students will learn how their daily choices and activities affect the environment. They will discover lifestyle changes that can help preserve the environment. As students gain more knowledge about "Going Green," they will implement the six Rs:

Reduce Refuse Reuse Recycle Research Respond

The students will learn to *reduce* trash, *refuse* excess packaging, *reuse* items, and *recycle.* They will also be encouraged to *research* and learn more about preserving the environment, and to *respond* by sharing their new learning with others.

Becoming more environmentally conscious is important. Many Earth-friendly choices benefit our health and well-being. Learning is the first step in making a positive difference in our world. Topics covered in *Going Green* will allow the students to discover choices they can make at school, which can extend to their homes and community.

Going Green's topic is an important environmental issue with its own terminology. Students are provided with key vocabulary words to help them better understand and discuss the concepts. Students absorb the information, think critically about the content, and discuss the material using authentic language. In each unit, suggestions and adaptations are provided for ELL students. Scaffolded activities provide all students with opportunities to read and research, and to demonstrate what they are learning in a variety of ways including graphic representations, writing, experimentation, and art.

Although progress has been made in "Going Green" since the first Earth Day in 1970, there is still much to do. The theme of this first global celebration was "Give Earth a Chance." It focused on the purity of air, water, and natural environments. Our society today still faces many environmental dilemmas. To enjoy Earth and its natural resources, we need to work together to take care of our environment. One group of students cannot solve all the problems overnight, but they can do their part. So let's give Earth a chance, one child at a time!

# How to Use This Book

This book has seven sections, typically with several lessons in each section. Each lesson has more than one part. You may want to teach one part each day, with an entire lesson covering approximately a week of class time. Doing so enables you to incorporate these environmental lessons into the existing curriculum in a busy classroom. Lessons meet cross-curricular standards and most include extensions.

The first section includes lessons that help students learn to "Think Green." Subsequent sections focus on the Rs of Going Green: Reduce, Refuse, Reuse, and Recycle. The Respond section helps the students respond to what they have learned (Research) and extend their learning beyond the classroom to their homes and community.

As you prepare to teach lessons, consider photocopying appropriate reproducible pages onto overhead transparencies or scanning them for an interactive whiteboard. The students may also use individual whiteboards to give responses in class. **Note:** When using individual whiteboards, the students need to be careful not to erase their responses accidentally.

As soon as possible, begin collecting magazine pictures related to the environment and natural resources to supplement lessons in this book. Specific lessons that use pictures include "Environmental Perspectives" (page 12), "Carbon Footprints" (page 27), "Energy Efficiency" (page 35), "Excessive Packaging" (page 56), "The Buzz on Batteries" (page 65), and "What Is Recycling?" (page 70).

Enlarge picture charts for classroom display if desired. Each lesson contains one or more tips, which you may find helpful to engage ELL students, students with special needs, or those who may need a little extra assistance.

Recycle Magazines Here

Animals   People   Homes Gardens   Other

Setting Up a Green Classroom

Use these ideas as a starting point to brainstorm and discuss what will work in your school or district.

Teach by Example

- Use recycled or reusable materials.
- Use a whiteboard and environmentally friendly whiteboard markers instead of handouts.
- Use PowerPoint® presentations for lessons.
- Involve students in discussions, rather than written reports, when possible.
- Use an online grading system to reduce paper.
- Turn off computers if away for longer than 30 minutes.
- Teach the students to spoon out or pump small amounts when using soap, hand sanitizer, and glue. Challenge them to use a little dab, not a big squirt!
- Use environmentally friendly cleaning materials and disinfectants. (Combine ¼ c. water and $\frac{1}{2}$ c. vinegar to make a basic disinfectant. Add tea tree essential oil or lemon essential oil if you wish.)
- Teach the students how to use and care for materials so they will last as long as possible.
- Place outlines and activity sheets in plastic page protectors, allowing the students to write with erasable markers and erase with a rag.
- Share a refrigerator with colleagues.
- Use your own mug.

A Greener Classroom

- Establish recycling areas and a scrap paper bin.
- Create a list of environmentally friendly school supplies and enlist parent help if possible. Here are a few ways to get started:
    - Buy *hand sanitizer* and *liquid soap* in bulk. That way, the pump, which doesn't recycle well, can be reused.
    - Buy *glue* in bulk. Use as small an amount as needed on Styrofoam meat trays, plastic lids, etc.
- Use recycled cans to hold classroom supplies including pencils, markers, student nametags, etc.
- Collect the plastic covers (cylinders) that come on containers of 100 CDs. Use these containers to store manipulatives and supplies. They make great planters and water containers, too.
- Make individual student whiteboards using shower board (available for purchase at home improvement stores).
- Use a non-electric pencil sharpener and sharpen pencils "the old-fashioned way." This builds muscles, too!
- Use both sides of paper (i.e., when writing in a notebook, journal, or on loose-leaf notebook paper).

Setting Up a Green Classroom *(cont.)*

Green Word Wall

Each lesson begins with a standards-based objective and includes pertinent vocabulary words or phrases that can be incorporated into daily language. It is suggested that featured words and phrases be written on leaves (made from paper scraps) to create a special Green Word Wall in the classroom. The intent is to familiarize students with the words and concepts.

For a Green Word Wall display, create a three-dimensional tree out of recycled Materials using recycled brown paper bags. Make small background leaves for the tree out of dark green construction-paper scraps. Write each vocabulary word or phrase on lighter green paper leaves. Add the new vocabulary leaves at the beginning of each lesson. Refer to the Green Word Wall often and refer to the Green vocabulary in discussions and other oral language activities.

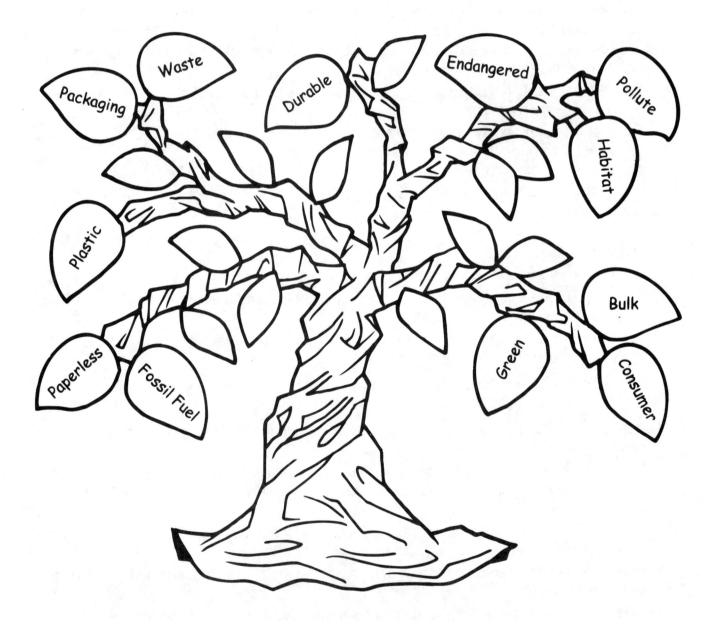

Standards and Benchmarks

Each lesson in *Going Green* meets at least one of the McREL standards and benchmarks, which are used with permission. Benchmarks are listed in parentheses after the lesson title. McREL, Mid-continent Research for Education and Learning, © 2009. Web site: *www.mcrel.org* Telephone: 303-337-0990.

Standards and Benchmarks	Title and Benchmarks
WRITING	
Standard 1. Uses the general skills and strategies of the writing process **Benchmark 1.** Prewriting: Uses prewriting strategies to plan written work (e.g., uses graphic organizers, story maps; groups related ideas; takes notes, brainstorms ideas; organizes information according to type and purpose of writing) **Benchmark 2.** Drafting and Revising: Uses strategies to draft and revise written work (e.g., elaborates on a central idea; writes with attention to audience, word choice, sentence variation; uses paragraphs to develop separate ideas; produces multiple drafts) **Benchmark 3.** Editing and Publishing: Uses strategies to edit and publish written work (e.g., edits for grammar, punctuation, capitalization, and spelling at a developmentally appropriate level; uses reference materials; considers page format [paragraphs, margins, indentations, titles]; selects presentation format according to purpose; incorporates photos, illustrations, charts, and graphs; uses available technology to compose and publish work) **Benchmark 5.** Uses strategies (e.g., adapts focus, organization, point of view; determines knowledge and interests of audience) to write for different audiences (e.g., self, peers, teachers, adults) **Benchmark 6.** Uses strategies (e.g., adapts focus, point of view, organization, form) to write for a variety of purposes (e.g., to inform, entertain, explain, describe, record ideas) **Benchmark 10.** Writes expressive compositions (e.g., expresses ideas, reflections, and observations; uses an individual, authentic voice; uses narrative strategies, relevant details, and ideas that enable the reader to imagine the world of the event or experience) **Benchmark 12.** Writes personal letters (i.e., includes the date, address, greeting, body, and closing; addresses envelopes, includes signature)	Environmental Perspectives (1) How to Go Green (6) Carbon Footprints (1) Heal the Planet (2, 10) New Ways of Thinking (1, 12) Excessive Packaging (10) Avoid Plastic (1) Lunchtime Rhymes (1) In the Community (1, 5) Trash to Treasure (1, 10) Precious Rainwater (6) Keep It Out of the Landfill (1, 6) Learn About Labels (1, 2, 3, 6) Living Green (1, 2, 5, 6)
Standard 2. Uses the stylistic and rhetorical aspects of writing **Benchmark 1.** Uses descriptive language that clarifies and enhances ideas (e.g., common figures of speech, sensory details) **Benchmark 2.** Uses paragraph form in writing (e.g., indents first word of a paragraph, uses topic sentences, recognizes a paragraph as a group of sentences about one main idea, uses an introductory and concluding paragraph, writes several related paragraphs) **Benchmark 3.** Uses a variety of sentence structures in writing (e.g., expands basic sentence patterns, uses exclamatory or imperative sentences)	Heal the Planet (3) Excessive Packaging (1) Trash to Treasure (1, 2, 3)
Standard 4. Gathers and uses information for research purposes **Benchmark 1.** Uses a variety of strategies to plan research (e.g., identifies possible topic by brainstorming, listing questions, using idea webs; organizes prior knowledge about a topic; develops a course of action; determines how to locate necessary information) **Benchmark 4.** Uses electronic media to gather information (e.g., databases, Internet, CD-ROM, television shows, cassette recordings, videos, pull-down menus, word searches) **Benchmark 5.** Uses key words, guide words, alphabetical and numerical order, indexes, cross-references, and letters on volumes to find information for research topics **Benchmark 7.** Uses strategies to gather and record information for research topics (e.g., uses notes, maps, charts, graphs, tables, and other graphic organizers; paraphrases and summarizes information; gathers direct quotes; provides narrative descriptions)	Hunt for the Green (1, 4, 5, 7) The Greenhouse Effect (7)
READING	
Standard 5. Uses the general skills and strategies of the reading process **Benchmark 2.** Establishes a purpose for reading (e.g., for information, for pleasure, to understand a specific viewpoint) **Benchmark 4.** Uses phonetic and structural analysis techniques, syntactic structure, and semantic context to decode unknown words (e.g., vowel patterns, complex word families, syllabication, root words, affixes) **Benchmark 5.** Uses a variety of context clues to decode unknown words (e.g., draws on earlier reading, reads ahead)	Environmental Perspectives (2) New Ways of Thinking (7) Avoid Plastic (2, 5, 6, 7) Hunt for the Green (2, 4, 5) Learn About Labels (2, 4, 6)

Standards and Benchmarks *(cont.)*

Standards and Benchmarks	Title and Benchmarks
READING *(cont.)*	
Standard 5. *(cont.)* **Benchmark 6.** Uses word reference materials (e.g., glossary, dictionary, thesaurus) to determine the meaning, pronunciation, and derivations of unknown words) **Benchmark 7.** Understands level-appropriate reading vocabulary (e.g., synonyms, antonyms, homophones, multi-meaning words)	Environmental Perspectives (2) New Ways of Thinking (7) Avoid Plastic (2, 5, 6, 7) Hunt for the Green (2, 4, 5) Learn About Labels (2, 4, 6)
Standard 7. Uses reading skills and strategies to understand and interpret a variety of informational texts **Benchmark 1.** Uses reading skills and strategies to understand a variety of informational texts (e.g., textbooks, biographical sketches, letters, diaries, directions, procedures, magazines) **Benchmark 5.** Summarizes and paraphrases information in texts (e.g., includes the main idea and significant supporting details of a reading selection) **Benchmark 6.** Uses prior knowledge and experience to understand and respond to new information	Environmental Perspectives (1, 6) Avoid Plastic (1, 5, 6) Hunt for the Green (1)
LISTENING AND SPEAKING	
Standard 8. Uses listening and speaking strategies for different purposes **Benchmark 1.** Contributes to group discussions **Benchmark 2.** Asks questions in class (e.g., when he or she is confused, to seek others' opinions and comments) **Benchmark 3.** Responds to questions and comments (e.g., gives reasons in support of opinions, responds to others' ideas) **Benchmark 4.** Listens to classmates and adults (e.g., does not interrupt, faces the speaker, asks questions, summarizes or paraphrases to confirm understanding, gives feedback, eliminates barriers to effective listening) **Benchmark 6.** Uses level-appropriate vocabulary in speech **Benchmark 7.** Makes basic oral presentations to class (e.g., uses subject-related information and vocabulary, includes content appropriate to the audience; relates ideas and observations; incorporates visual aids or props; incorporates several sources of information) **Benchmark 8.** Uses a variety of nonverbal communication skills (e.g., eye contact, gestures, facial expressions, posture) **Benchmark 9.** Uses a variety of verbal communication skills (e.g., projection, tone, volume, rate, articulation, pace, phrasing) **Benchmark 11.** Listens for specific information in spoken texts (e.g., plot details or information about a character in a short story read aloud, information about a familiar topic from a radio broadcast) **Benchmark 15.** Knows specific ways in which language is used in real-life situations (e.g., buying something from a shopkeeper, requesting something from a parent, arguing with a sibling, talking to a friend)	How to Go Green (1) Heal the Planet (2, 3) New Ways of Thinking (1) Why Reduce Garbage? (4, 11) Lunchtime Rhymes (7, 8, 9, 15) In the Community (2, 3) Trash to Treasure (1) The Buzz on Batteries (3, 11) What Is Recycling? (1) Old Glass to New Product (1, 2, 6) Learn About Labels (1, 4)
MEDIA	
Standard 9. Uses viewing skills and strategies to understand and interpret visual media **Benchmark 6.** Understands the use and meaning of symbols and images in visual media (e.g., the use of color, such as red to represent emotion, anger, or excitement; the use of expressions, such as smiling to mean happiness; the dependence of symbols on shared social and cultural understandings; symbolic links between product names or logos and products) **Benchmark 7.** Understands basic elements of advertising in visual media (e.g., sales approaches and techniques aimed at children, appealing elements used in memorable commercials, possible reasons for the choice of specific visual images)	Excessive Packaging (7) The Buzz on Batteries (6) Learn About Labels (6)

8

Standards and Benchmarks	Title and Benchmarks
SCIENCE	
Standard 1. Understands atmospheric processes and the water cycle **Benchmark 1.** Knows that water exists in the air in different forms (e.g., in clouds and fog as tiny droplets; in rain, snow, and hail); and changes from one form to another through various processes (e.g., freezing, condensation, precipitation, evaporation) **Benchmark 3.** Knows that air is a substance that surrounds us, takes up space, and moves around us as wind	Heal the Planet (3) Precious Rainwater (1) The Greenhouse Effect (3)
Standard 2. Understands Earth's composition and structure **Benchmark 1.** Knows how features on Earth's surface are constantly changed by a combination of slow and rapid processes (e.g., slow processes, such as weathering, erosion, transport, and deposition of sediment caused by waves, wind, water, and ice; rapid processes, such as landslides, volcanic eruptions, and earthquakes)	Carbon Footprints (1)
Standard 6. Understands relationships among organisms and their physical environment **Benchmark 3.** Knows that an organism's patterns of behavior are related to the nature of that organism's environment (e.g., kinds and numbers of other organisms present, availability of food and resources, physical characteristics of the environment) **Benchmark 5.** Knows that all organisms (including humans) cause changes in their environments, and these changes can be beneficial or detrimental	Environmental Perspectives (3, 5) How to Go Green (5)
Standard 8. Understands the structure and properties of matter **Benchmark 1.** Knows that matter has different states (i.e., solid, liquid, gas) and that each state has distinct physical properties; some common materials such as water can be changed from one state to another by heating or cooling	Hunt for the Green (1)
Standard 9. Understands the sources and properties of energy **Benchmark 1.** Knows that heat is often produced as a byproduct when one form of energy is converted to another form (e.g., when machines and living organisms convert stored energy to motion) **Benchmark 2.** Knows that heat can move from one object to another by conduction and that some materials conduct heat better than others	Carbon Footprints (1) Energy Efficiency (1) The Buzz on Batteries (1, 2)
Standard 11. Understands the nature of scientific knowledge **Benchmark 5.** Understands that models (e.g., physical, conceptual, mathematical models, computer simulations) can be used to represent and predict changes in objects, events, and processes	Old Glass to New Product (5)
Standard 12. Understands the nature of scientific inquiry **Benchmark 3.** Plans and conducts simple investigations (e.g., formulates a testable question, plans a fair test, makes systematic observations, develops logical conclusions)	Energy Efficiency (3)
GEOGRAPHY	
Standard 14. Understands how human actions modify the physical environment **Benchmark 1.** Knows the ways people alter the physical environment (e.g., by creating irrigation projects; clearing the land to make room for houses and shopping centers; planting crops; building roads) **Benchmark 2.** Knows the ways in which the physical environment is stressed by human activities (e.g., changes in climate, air pollution, water pollution, expanding human settlement)	Environmental Perspectives (2) How to Go Green (2) Carbon Footprints (1, 2) Why Reduce Garbage? (1, 2) Lunchtime Rhymes (1) Keep It Out of the Landfill (2) Learn About Labels (1, 2) Living Green (1, 2)

Standards and Benchmarks	Title and Benchmarks
GEOGRAPHY *(cont.)*	
Standard 16. Understands the changes that occur in the meaning, use, distribution, and importance of resources **Benchmark 1.** Knows the characteristics, location, and use of renewable resources (e.g., timber), flow resources (e.g., running water or wind), and nonrenewable resources (e.g., fossil fuels, minerals) **Benchmark 3.** Knows the relationship between economic activities and resources (e.g., the relationship of major industrial districts to the location of iron ore, coal, and other resources) **Benchmark 5.** Knows advantages and disadvantages of recycling and reusing different types of materials	Environmental Perspectives (5) How to Go Green (5) Carbon Footprints (1) Why Reduce Garbage? (5) Lunchtime Rhymes (5) The Buzz on Batteries (5) Precious Rainwater (1, 5) What Is Recycling? (5) Hunt for the Green (5) Old Glass to New Product (5) Keep It Out of the Landfill (5) Learn About Labels (3, 5) Living Green (5)
SOCIAL STUDIES—BEHAVIOR	
Standard 1. Understands that group and cultural influences contribute to human development, identity, and behavior **Benchmark 1.** Understands that people can learn about others in many different ways (e.g, direct experience, mass communications media, conversations with others about their work and lives)	Learn About Labels (1) Living Green (1)
Standard 3. Understands that interactions among learning, inheritance, and physical development affect human behavior **Benchmark 5.** Knows that learning means using what one already knows to make sense out of new experiences or information, not just storing the new information in one's head	Learn About Labels (5) Living Green (5)
HEALTH	
Standard 2. Knows environmental and external factors that affect individual and community health **Benchmark 2.** Knows how individuals, communities, and states cooperate to control environmental problems and maintain a healthy environment	Lunchtime Rhymes (2)
MATH	
Standard 4. Understands and applies basic and advanced properties of the concepts of measurement **Benchmark 2.** Selects and uses appropriate tools for given measurement situations (e.g., rulers for length, measuring cups for capacity, protractors for angle) **Benchmark 6.** Uses specific strategies to estimate quantities and measurements (e.g., estimating the whole by estimating the parts)	Precious Rainwater (2, 6)
Standard 6. Understands and applies basic and advanced concepts of statistics and data analysis **Benchmark 4.** Organizes and displays data in simple bar graphs, pie charts, and line graphs **Benchmark 5.** Reads and interprets simple bar graphs, pie charts, and line graphs	Energy Efficiency (4, 5) The Greenhouse Effect (4, 5)
VISUAL ARTS	
Standard 1. Understands and applies media, techniques, and processes related to the visual arts **Benchmark 3.** Knows how different media (e.g., oil, watercolor, stone, metal), techniques, and processes are used to communicate ideas, experiences, and stories	What Is Recycling? (3)
THEATER	
Standard 2. Uses acting skills **Benchmark 2.** Uses variations of locomotor and non-locomotor movement and vocal pitch, tempo, and tone for different characters	In the Community (2)

Going Green!

Date: _____

Dear Parent or Guardian:

This year our class is learning how to "Go Green" and make choices that help the environment. Adopting environmentally friendly behaviors involves new ways of thinking.

The students will focus on ways our class can become more "green." They will learn to *reduce* trash, *refuse* excess packaging, *reuse* items, and *recycle*. The students will also be encouraged to *research* and learn more about preserving the environment, and they will learn to *respond* by sharing their new learning with others.

Scientists have raised awareness and concerns about environmental issues, such as nonrenewable energy sources, negative effects of using fossil fuels on the atmosphere and climate, and harmful effects of pollution on plant and animal life. To enjoy Earth and its natural resources, we need to work together to take care of our environment.

One group of students cannot solve all these problems overnight, but they can do their part. Similarly, we do not expect one family to be able to incorporate all the ideas and suggestions that students will discuss in class. We hope that you will talk with your child about what he or she is learning and will make the effort to make a few of these practices part of your life. One simple way to "Go Green" is to turn off the lights when leaving a room.

Thank you for supporting our efforts,

_____

Note to Teacher: Scan this letter to be sent as an e-mail if possible.

Environmental Perspectives

Objective: Given an example from nature, the students will think about their perspectives and concerns about the environment and participate in creating a class bulletin board display.

Vocabulary

- environment
- environmentally friendly
- Green
- perspective

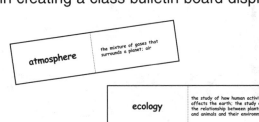

atmosphere	the mixture of gases that surrounds a planet; air

ecology	the study of how human activity affects the earth; the study of the relationship between plants and animals and their environment

Materials

- "Eagles" passage below (Level 3.9)
- Environmental Words and Definitions Cards on pages 14–17
- overhead projector, chart paper or interactive whiteboard, and appropriate markers
- 3-D eagle figurine or picture
- sheet of white paper for each group
- two 3" x 5" index cards or pieces of cardstock for each student (eco-friendlier option: heavy scrap paper)

Preparation

1. Copy the Environmental Words and Definitions and the "Eagles" passage below onto a transparency or scan them into an interactive whiteboard.
2. Fold back the definitions for the Environmental Words. Tape or glue the cards together.

Opening

1. Introduce this unit of study by telling the students they will learn how to take better care of the environment. Ask the students how they would define the word *environment*. (natural world of land, sea, and air, including plants and animals)
2. Define the word *perspective*. Explain that the way people look at things is their perspective.
3. Display the eagle figurine. Discuss how a person's or animal's perspective is the way they view a particular situation or the world around them. As an example, have the students describe an eagle's perspective on the world. (They soar above water and fields to hunt.)
4. Continue the class discussion by having student volunteers read the following information.

Eagles

Eagles have excellent eyesight. They can see forward and to the side at the same time. This gives them more than one perspective. When soaring or gliding, they can see fish in the water below. A young eagle may make a mistake and attack a plastic bottle floating in the water instead of a fish.

Eagles often eat dead fish. Fish are dark colored on top and light colored underneath. Dead fish float belly up. This makes it easier for the eagle to see them from above as they fly.

Eagles see in color. Their vision is sharper than that of humans. They can spot moving prey, such as a rabbit moving, from a great distance.

Environmental Perspectives *(cont.)*

Part 1

1. Explain that, like eagles, people have different ways of viewing the world. We do not all have the same perspectives or concerns about the environment.

2. Divide the students into groups of four or five students each. Give each group a sheet of white paper. Have each group use a web or another type of graphic organizer to take notes as they discuss their perspectives and concerns about the environment. For example, the students might discuss their thoughts on recycling or reusing items. They might say that they have not thought about the environment before. They might wonder what our world will be like in 20 or 30 years when fuel resources become less available.

3. Direct the students to make their webs legible, as they will be used as part of a display.

Part 2

1. Expand the students' thinking by asking them what the term "Go Green" means. Explain that people use the words *Green* and *environmentally friendly* to describe something that is good for the environment. Some things we do help the environment, and other things we do harm the environment.

2. Brainstorm a list of Green ideas. Write them on the overhead or whiteboard.

3. Explain that students can take care of the environment by adapting the way they live and do things—beginning in the classroom. Tell the students that in these lessons they will learn how their daily choices and activities affect the environment. They will learn to make changes in how they do things that will help preserve the environment.

Part 3

1. Introduce the Environmental Words and Definitions Cards to students without showing the definitions.

2. Give each student two index cards. Assign one word to each student and direct him or her to look up the definition of the word. Provide assistance as needed to find Green definitions or suggest the definition provided.

3. Have each student create a word card and a definition card for his or her word.

4. Have students use the cards to play a matching card game, similar to Concentration.

Closing

1. Have the groups share their webs with the class. Work together as a class to create a classroom bulletin board display.

2. Ask the students how their views and understanding of the environment have changed after discussing this topic in small groups and as a whole class.

ELL Tip

Use motions to act out the different perspectives of an eagle (side, front, looking down, gazing straight ahead). Help the students understand how they have different perspectives on the topic of the environment.

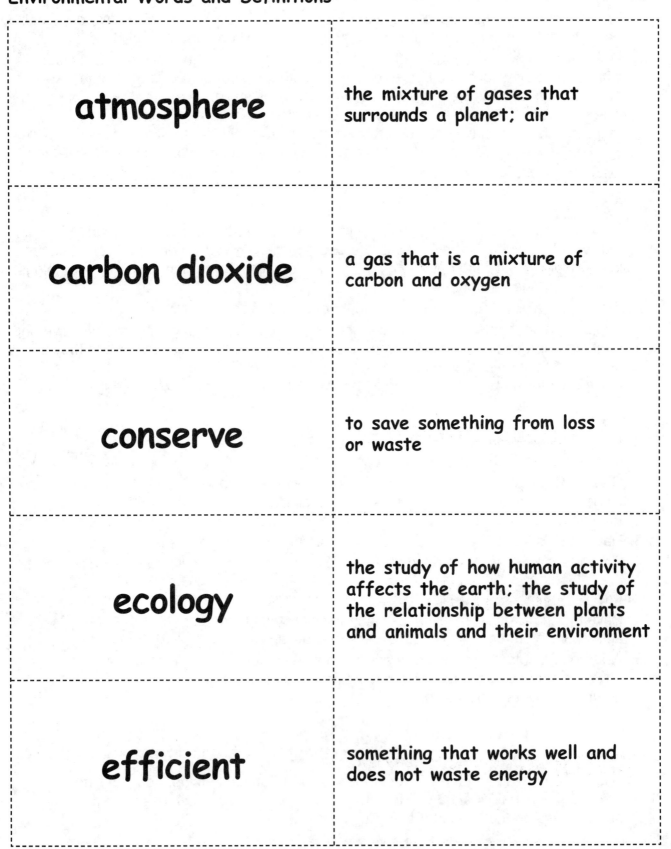 Environmental Perspectives (cont.)

Environmental Words and Definitions

atmosphere	the mixture of gases that surrounds a planet; air
carbon dioxide	a gas that is a mixture of carbon and oxygen
conserve	to save something from loss or waste
ecology	the study of how human activity affects the earth; the study of the relationship between plants and animals and their environment
efficient	something that works well and does not waste energy

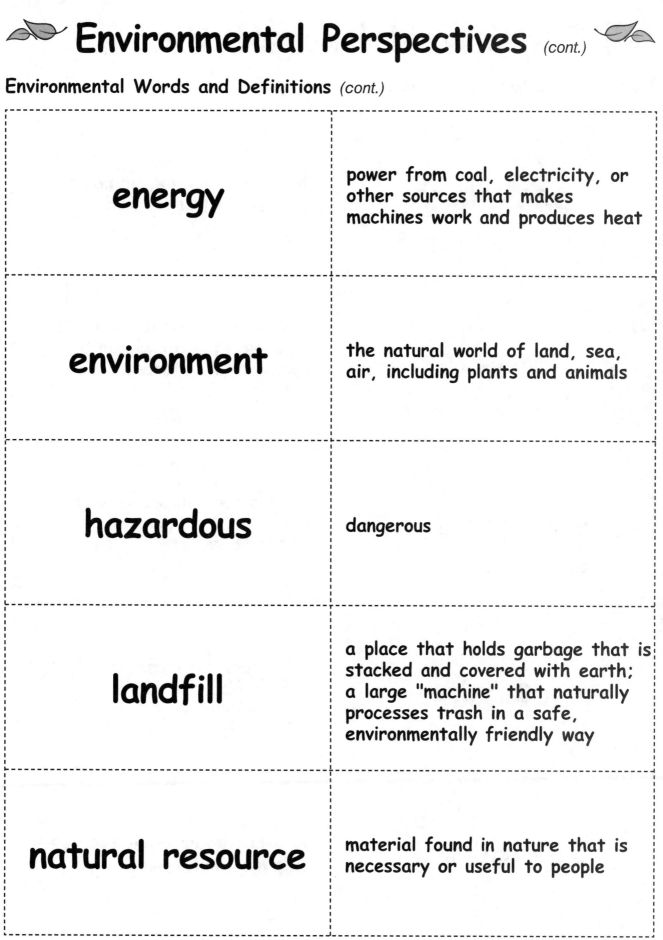 Environmental Perspectives (cont.)

Environmental Words and Definitions (cont.)

energy	power from coal, electricity, or other sources that makes machines work and produces heat
environment	the natural world of land, sea, air, including plants and animals
hazardous	dangerous
landfill	a place that holds garbage that is stacked and covered with earth; a large "machine" that naturally processes trash in a safe, environmentally friendly way
natural resource	material found in nature that is necessary or useful to people

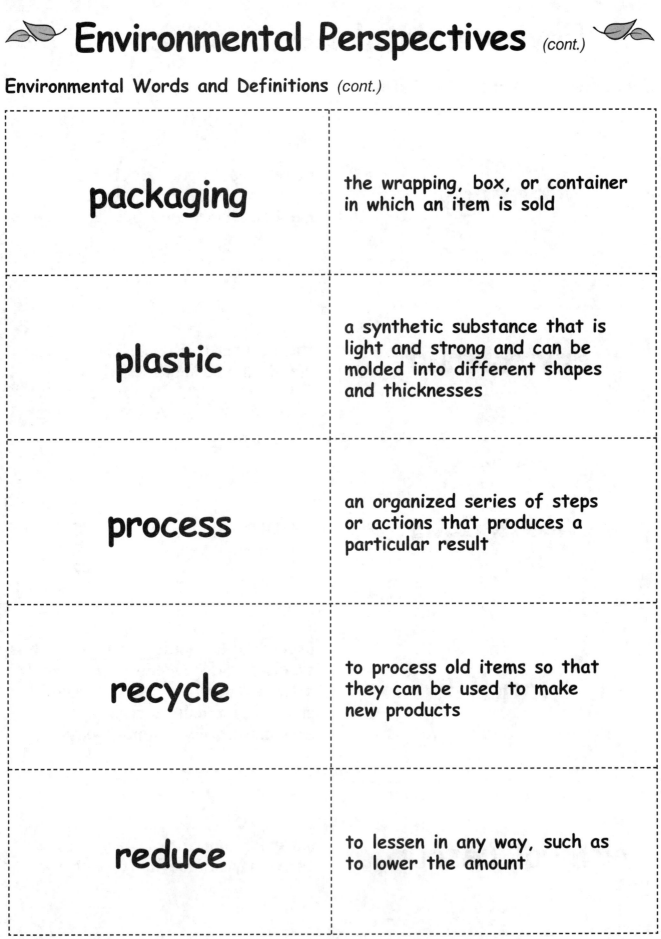 Environmental Perspectives (cont.)

Environmental Words and Definitions (cont.)

packaging	the wrapping, box, or container in which an item is sold
plastic	a synthetic substance that is light and strong and can be molded into different shapes and thicknesses
process	an organized series of steps or actions that produces a particular result
recycle	to process old items so that they can be used to make new products
reduce	to lessen in any way, such as to lower the amount

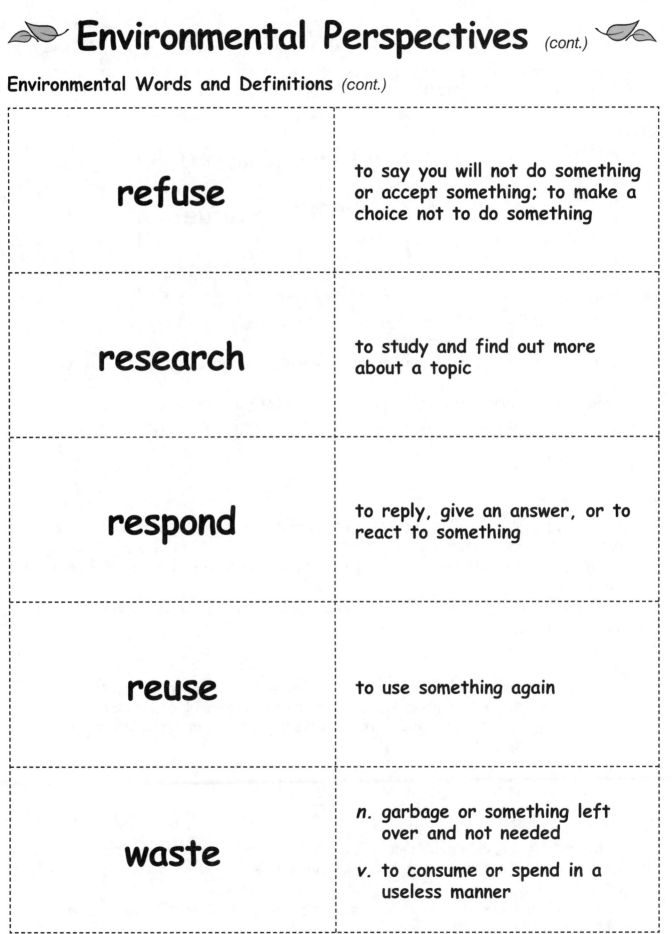

Environmental Perspectives *(cont.)*

Environmental Words and Definitions *(cont.)*

refuse	to say you will not do something or accept something; to make a choice not to do something
research	to study and find out more about a topic
respond	to reply, give an answer, or to react to something
reuse	to use something again
waste	*n.* garbage or something left over and not needed *v.* to consume or spend in a useless manner

How to Go Green

Objective: Given an introduction to key words used in environmental concerns, the students will design posters showing symbols for the R words to display in the classroom.

Vocabulary

- reduce
- refuse
- reuse
- recycle
- research
- respond

> Reduce Research
> Reuse Refuse
> Recycle Respond

Materials

- Becoming G-R-R-R-R-R-EEN—Learn the Rs on pages 20–21
- What Students Can Do miniposter on page 22
- overhead projector, chart paper or interactive whiteboard, and appropriate green marker
- 7 pieces of poster board
  (eco-friendlier option: pieces of light-colored, lightweight cardboard)
- sheet of white construction paper or cardstock for each student (optional)
- markers
- Glossary on pages 93–96

Preparation

1. Prepare Becoming G-R-R-R-R-R-EEN—Learn the Rs as a poster for a classroom display. Use posterboard or colored paper.
2. Read through the prepared poster to become familiar with how each word contributes to the idea of Going Green.
3. Copy the What Students Can Do miniposter onto an overhead or scan into an interactive whiteboard.

Opening

1. Write six large Rs with a green marker on the whiteboard or transparency. Ask the students what these Rs might stand for in an environmentally friendly classroom. If the students suggest the words *reduce, reuse,* or *recycle,* ask them how these words are related to the environment.
2. Have the students give definitions for any related R words they suggest.
3. Go over the definitions for the remaining R words as listed in the Glossary.

Part 1

1. Show the students the What Students Can Do miniposter on the overhead or whiteboard. Refer to Learn the Rs to discuss how each R word contributes to taking care of the environment.
2. Encourage student participation to increase their understanding of the words and concepts related to going Green.

How to Go Green *(cont.)*

Part 2

1. Divide the students into six groups. Each group will focus on one R word. Randomly assign a word to each group.
2. Distribute poster board and markers to each group.
3. Each group will design a poster depicting their topic for a classroom display.
4. Remind the students to first brainstorm ideas on scratch paper from the recycling bin and use pencil and eraser when arranging their design on the poster.
5. Encourage the students to use creativity and neatness.

Closing

1. Have the groups present their posters and explain the symbols to the class.
2. Display the posters in the class as visual reminders to "Go Green" and practice environmentally friendly activities.

Extension

Have the students choose one of the six R words discussed and work individually to design a poster on construction paper or cardstock. Display the individual student posters, grouped by topic. Conduct a class discussion about the environmental messages conveyed on the posters.

ELL Tip

Use the following sentence starters to reinforce the six new R vocabulary words. Allow time for further discussion to assist the students in completing the sentences.

I can **recycle** _____ .

I can **reduce** garbage by _____ .

When you **reuse** something, you are _____ .

I will **refuse** to _____ .

I want to **research** to learn more about _____ .

I can **respond** and share what I have learned with _____

_____ .

Becoming G-R-R-R-R-R-R-EEN

Reduce

If you don't need it, don't buy it.

Why?
- ⊕ Many man-made items do not biodegrade (break down).
- ⊕ Trash stays in landfills for a long time.

Alternative: Do you really need a new backpack? Can you use the backpack from last year?

Refuse

Don't buy things that have too much packaging. Look for more Earth-friendly packaging solutions. Try to avoid items packaged in "clam shells." Don't buy items that cannot be recycled unless it is absolutely necessary.

Why?
- ⊕ The packaging generates more trash for landfills.
- ⊕ It takes energy to make new products and the packaging needed to sell them.
- ⊕ We get much of our energy from nonrenewable resources.
- ⊕ Using energy can pollute Earth.

Alternatives: Instead of having individually wrapped cheese sticks for an after-school snack, ask to cut sticks from a larger block of cheese. Individually wrapped snack foods have extra packaging. Choose crayons or markers that come in cardboard boxes, which can be recycled, instead of plastic wrappers or containers that cannot be recycled. Make birthday gifts or cards instead of buying new, packaged items.

Reuse

Find new uses for items that no longer fit or are of interest, instead of throwing them away.

Why?
- ⊕ The item will become trash and go in the landfill.
- ⊕ You won't need to spend money for something new.

Alternatives: If you cannot recycle a torn plastic folder, use the pieces of the folder in the bottom of a cloth bag to make it sturdier. If you have outgrown your jeans and they are too short, cut them off and make shorts or capris.

Learn the Rs

Recycle

Sort bottles, cans, paper, plastic, etc., and recycle to convert them, rather than fill a landfill.

Why?
⊕ Making new items requires huge amounts of energy (electricity).
⊕ Recycling takes less energy and uses fewer resources.

Alternatives: Recycle plastic milk jugs. They can be made into park benches and playground equipment. Recycle paper, it might be used to make the next book you read.

Research

Learn more about environmentally friendly products.

Why?
⊕ Be part of the solution, not part of the problem.
⊕ Support companies that want to take care of the environment.
⊕ Learn how to take better care of Earth.

Alternative: Ask an adult to help you use the Internet or the library to learn about Earth-friendly packaging.

Respond

Share with others what you have learned about helping the environment.

Why?
⊕ More people can do environmentally friendly things.
⊕ More people can purchase items with environmentally friendly packaging.

Alternatives: I can tell my parents what I learn about recycling and help recycle things at home.
I can remind my friends not to litter or waste water.

What Students Can Do

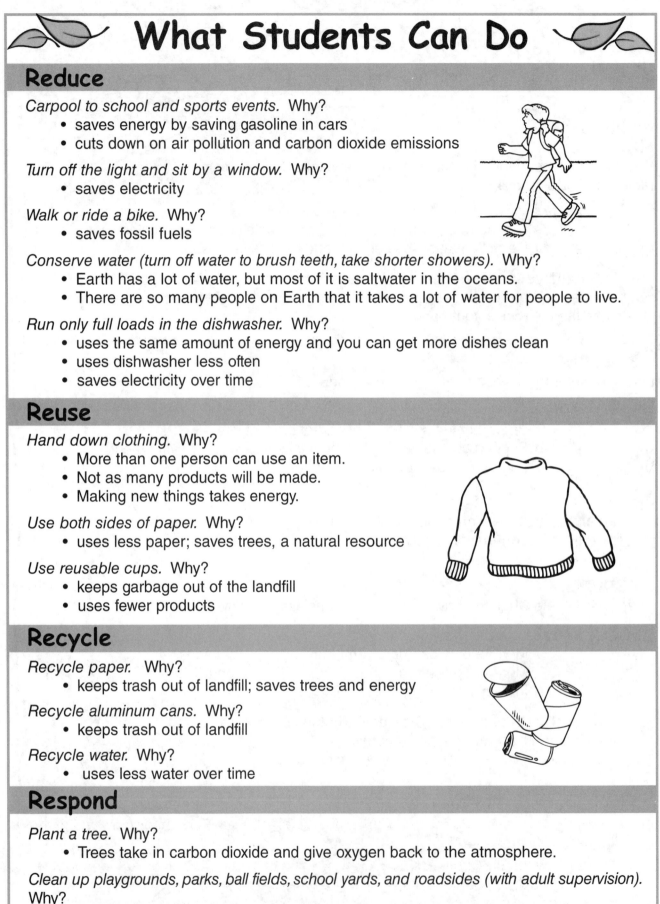

Reduce

Carpool to school and sports events. Why?
- saves energy by saving gasoline in cars
- cuts down on air pollution and carbon dioxide emissions

Turn off the light and sit by a window. Why?
- saves electricity

Walk or ride a bike. Why?
- saves fossil fuels

Conserve water (turn off water to brush teeth, take shorter showers). Why?
- Earth has a lot of water, but most of it is saltwater in the oceans.
- There are so many people on Earth that it takes a lot of water for people to live.

Run only full loads in the dishwasher. Why?
- uses the same amount of energy and you can get more dishes clean
- uses dishwasher less often
- saves electricity over time

Reuse

Hand down clothing. Why?
- More than one person can use an item.
- Not as many products will be made.
- Making new things takes energy.

Use both sides of paper. Why?
- uses less paper; saves trees, a natural resource

Use reusable cups. Why?
- keeps garbage out of the landfill
- uses fewer products

Recycle

Recycle paper. Why?
- keeps trash out of landfill; saves trees and energy

Recycle aluminum cans. Why?
- keeps trash out of landfill

Recycle water. Why?
- uses less water over time

Respond

Plant a tree. Why?
- Trees take in carbon dioxide and give oxygen back to the atmosphere.

Clean up playgrounds, parks, ball fields, school yards, and roadsides (with adult supervision). Why?
- Litter is harmful to plants and animals.

Learn About Labels

Objective: Given an introduction to recycling symbols, the students will create a brochure to increase consumer awareness about recycling.

Vocabulary

- consumer
- fiber
- post-consumer waste
- pre-consumer waste

Materials

- Seals and Symbols on pages 25–26
- overhead projector, chart paper or interactive whiteboard, and appropriate markers
- sample informational brochures
- sheet of white construction paper for each student (eco-friendlier option: access to slide show software, e.g., PowerPoint™)
- markers or colored pencils
- cardstock
- sample product items or packaging with recycle labels (e.g., wrapping from a package of computer paper, box of envelopes) (optional)

Preparation

1. Copy the Seals and Symbols onto cardstock. Cut them apart to make cards. Each student should have one card.
2. Copy the Seals and Symbols pages onto a transparency or scan it into an interactive whiteboard for class display.
3. Gather a display of informational brochures to show the students the layout of a brochure (bi-fold or tri-fold, includes pictures and text, gives information).

Opening

1. Ask the students to raise their hands if they are *consumers*. Explain that each of them is a consumer because they buy or use products and services.
2. Ask the students to name a material that is made from wood. Tell the students that and paper is made from wood and it contains plant fibers.
3. Define a *fiber* as a long, thin thread of material, such as cotton or wool, which comes from a plant.
4. Review with the students how the prefix *post-* changes the meaning of a word to include the idea of "after." Write the term and definition of *post-consumer waste* on the overhead or whiteboard. (contains materials people have already used and thrown away; the things that have been recycled)
5. Discuss how the prefix *pre-* changes the meaning of a word to include the idea that something happens before something else. Write the term and definition of *pre-consumer material* on the overhead or whiteboard. (waste from the manufacturing process, before people have used the product)

Learn About Labels *(cont.)*

Part 1

1. Discuss with the students items that have recycling symbols or seals on them. Ask the students where they have seen an environmentel label or symbol on a product (e.g., plastic wrap, cardboard packaging, plastic water bottle). Tell the students that some symbols explain how much of the product comes from recycled material (e.g., tissue box, plastic sandwich box, foil carton) or from recycled fibers (e.g., napkins, paper towels, tissue).

2. Display the Seals and Symbols cards on the overhead or whiteboard. Point out the following cards and list examples of where each can be found:
   - **Green Seal**—*copy paper, envelopes*
   - **Energy Star**—*refrigerator, microwave, dishwasher*
   - **Forest Stewardship Council**—*wood products*
   - **Sustainable Forestry Initiative**—*computer paper packaging*
   - **USDA Certified Organic**—*cotton, dairy, poultry, eggs*

Part 2

1. Randomly distribute the Seals and Symbols cards to the students. Group students with like cards together.

2. Have the students discuss with their groups the meaning of the symbols and seals. Encourage each group to make a list of products on which they might see one of the featured seals and symbols. Allow research as needed.

3. Have the groups share their findings with the class.

Part 3

1. Have the students use construction paper and markers or computer software to create a brochure to increase consumer awareness about recycling labels on products.

2. The students should include more than one symbol on their brochure.

Closing

1. Review the vocabulary terms (*consumer*, *fiber*, *pre-consumer waste*, and *post-consumer waste*) with the students and encourage them to use the terms to explain the brochures to family members.

2. Have the students take their brochures home to share with family members. Encourage them to apply their learning about recycling and recycling symbols to help family members make environmentally friendly purchasing decisions.

Extension

As a class, create a PowerPoint™ presentation to show at a school assembly or parent night.

ELL Tip

Show the students sample product labels as each symbol is discussed in class. Review definitions for each symbol in a small group if necessary.

Learn About Labels (cont.)

Seals and Symbols

	Green Seal Green Seal™ is a non-profit organization dedicated to protecting the environment and human health. Founded in 1989, Green Seal develops standards based on environmental and human impacts as well as performance. You can find the Green Seal on a range of certified products and services from hotels and cleaning services to papers and paints. *http://www.greenseal.org*
	Energy Star ENERGY STAR is a government program that helps us all save money and protect the environment through energy efficient products and practices. In 2008, Americans—with the help of ENERGY STAR—saved $19 billion on their energy bills and avoided greenhouse gas emissions equivalent to 29 million cars. *http://www.energystar.gov*
	Forest Stewardship Council (FSC) The Forest Stewardship Council was established in 1993 and is represented in over 82 countries. It is an independent, not-for-profit organization. The FSC label can be found on timber, paper, and other forest products. FSC strives to create a marketplace that promotes well-managed forests by ensuring forestry practices that are environmentally responsible, socially beneficial, and economically viable. *http://www.fsc.org*
	Sustainable Forestry Initiative (SFI) SFI Inc. is an independent non-profit program dedicated to promoting responsible forest management in the United States and Canada through its forest management standards and throughout the world with its unique requirements for purchasing wood fiber from other suppliers. The SFI program labels are found on wood and paper products. The SFI label is a sign you are buying products from a responsible source, backed by a rigorous third-party audit. *http://www.sfiprogram.org*

Learn About Labels *(cont.)*

Seals and Symbols *(cont.)*

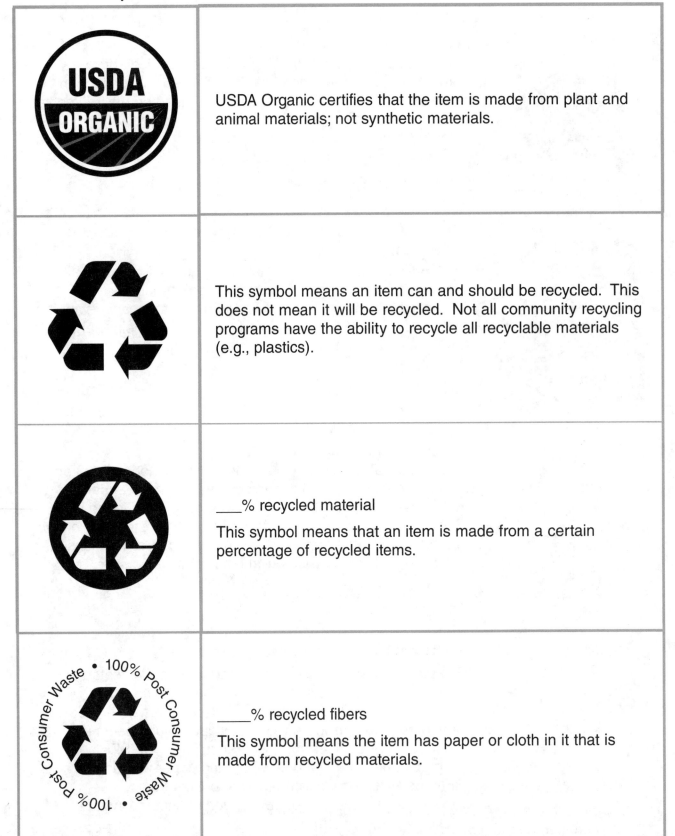

USDA Organic certifies that the item is made from plant and animal materials; not synthetic materials.

This symbol means an item can and should be recycled. This does not mean it will be recycled. Not all community recycling programs have the ability to recycle all recyclable materials (e.g., plastics).

___% recycled material

This symbol means that an item is made from a certain percentage of recycled items.

_____% recycled fibers

This symbol means the item has paper or cloth in it that is made from recycled materials.

Carbon Footprints

Objective: Given information about activities that are beneficial or not beneficial for the environment, the students will identify their own "carbon footprints."

Vocabulary

- carbon dioxide
- carbon footprint
- emission
- fossil fuel

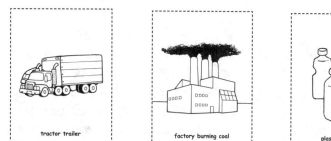 

tractor trailer

factory burning coal

plastic bottles

Materials

- Carbon Dioxide and Carbon Footprints on page 29
- Carbon Footprint Picture Cards on pages 30–31
- overhead projector, chalkboard or interactive whiteboard, and appropriate markers
- large world map (eco-friendlier option: make a map using an old shower curtain)
- sheet of brown construction paper for each student (eco-friendlier option: reuse brown paper bags)
- tacks or tape
- scissors
- markers or crayons
- magazine pictures (optional)

Preparation

1. Preview Carbon Dioxide and Carbon Footprints.
2. If using a shower curtain, have the students, older students from another class, or parent volunteers help paint or draw a simple world image and set aside to dry.
3. Copy a class set of Carbon Footprint Picture Cards and cut them apart.
4. Have the students color the picture cards for use during the lesson.

Opening

1. Define *fossil fuel.* Fuel is something that burns, like coal, oil, or gas. A fossil fuel is fuel that is formed from the remains of fossils, or prehistoric plants and animals.
2. Ask the students if anyone knows what *carbon dioxide* is. (Carbon dioxide a gas that is a mixture of carbon and oxygen.) Remind the students that people breathe in oxygen to keep them alive. They breathe out carbon dioxide.
3. Explain that carbon dioxide enters the air in other ways. We call this a carbon dioxide *emission* because it is a substance going into the air.
4. Other activities that give off carbon dioxide emissions include burning fossil fuels (coal, natural gas) for transportation, industry, and manufacturing, and generating electricity.

Part 1

1. Review the concept that plants and oceans remove carbon dioxide from the atmosphere. Plants give oxygen back into the air as they convert energy from the sun into food.
2. Explain to the students that, when there are more carbon dioxide emissions than available sources to absorb the carbon dioxide, it upsets the natural balance.

Carbon Footprints *(cont.)*

Part 2

1. Draw a large footprint on the board. Tell the students that this represents a "carbon footprint." A *carbon footprint* shows how much carbon dioxide gas goes into the air from things people do every day.

2. Place one picture card at a time on the footprint. Discuss how each contributes to levels of carbon dioxide in the atmosphere.
   - Many factories generate electricity by burning fossil fuels (coal, oil, and natural gas), which increases levels of carbon dioxide in the atmosphere.
   - Transportation and manufacturers of materials, particularly plastic, also rely on fossil fuels.

3. Give each student a sheet of brown paper. Have each student trace a foot on the paper. The students should keep their shoes on and may add toes once they have the general shape traced.

4. Direct the students to write things they do each day that add to their carbon footprint. Suggest activities that contribute to carbon dioxide emissions, such as the following:
   - riding in a car to school instead of walking or riding a bike
   - watching TV or playing video games after school instead of playing or reading a book

5. Younger students may glue magazine pictures on their footprints to depict activities that contribute to carbon dioxide emissions.

Part 3

1. Have the students temporarily attach their footprints to the world map using tacks or tape.

2. Generate a class chart of reminders, listing things the students can do to "reduce" their carbon footprint.

3. Every time a student acts in a way that reduces his or her carbon footprint (turns off lights when leaving a room, reuses or recycles something instead of throwing it away, uses less electricity), he or she may use scissors to trim a small piece off his or her footprint.

Closing

1. Work with students to create and label a diagram, showing the role of carbon dioxide in the atmosphere as explained in the Opening discussion.

2. The students should include plants, people, and other things or activities related to carbon dioxide emissions. Remind them to label their diagrams.

Extension

Encourage the students to do things at home to reduce their carbon footprints. For example, the students can turn off lights when not in use. The students may bring notes from home about what they did and then trim off a bit of their carbon footprints.

ELL Tip

Pair each student with a native speaker to create simple word webs of the vocabulary words. For example, have the students write *fossil fuels* in the center of a web. On branches of the web, have them list types of fossil fuels such as coal, oil, and natural gas.

Carbon Dioxide and Carbon Footprints

Carbon Dioxide

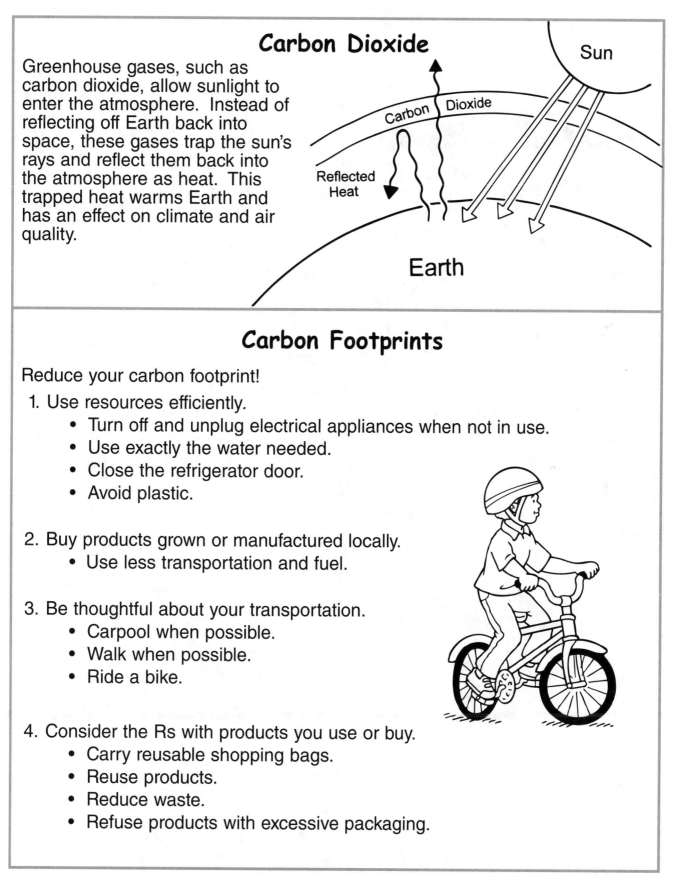

Greenhouse gases, such as carbon dioxide, allow sunlight to enter the atmosphere. Instead of reflecting off Earth back into space, these gases trap the sun's rays and reflect them back into the atmosphere as heat. This trapped heat warms Earth and has an effect on climate and air quality.

Sun

Carbon Dioxide

Reflected Heat

Earth

Carbon Footprints

Reduce your carbon footprint!

1. Use resources efficiently.
   - Turn off and unplug electrical appliances when not in use.
   - Use exactly the water needed.
   - Close the refrigerator door.
   - Avoid plastic.

2. Buy products grown or manufactured locally.
   - Use less transportation and fuel.

3. Be thoughtful about your transportation.
   - Carpool when possible.
   - Walk when possible.
   - Ride a bike.

4. Consider the Rs with products you use or buy.
   - Carry reusable shopping bags.
   - Reuse products.
   - Reduce waste.
   - Refuse products with excessive packaging.

Carbon Footprint Picture Cards

factory burning coal

plastic bottles

car

tractor trailer

30

Carbon Footprint Picture Cards *(cont.)*

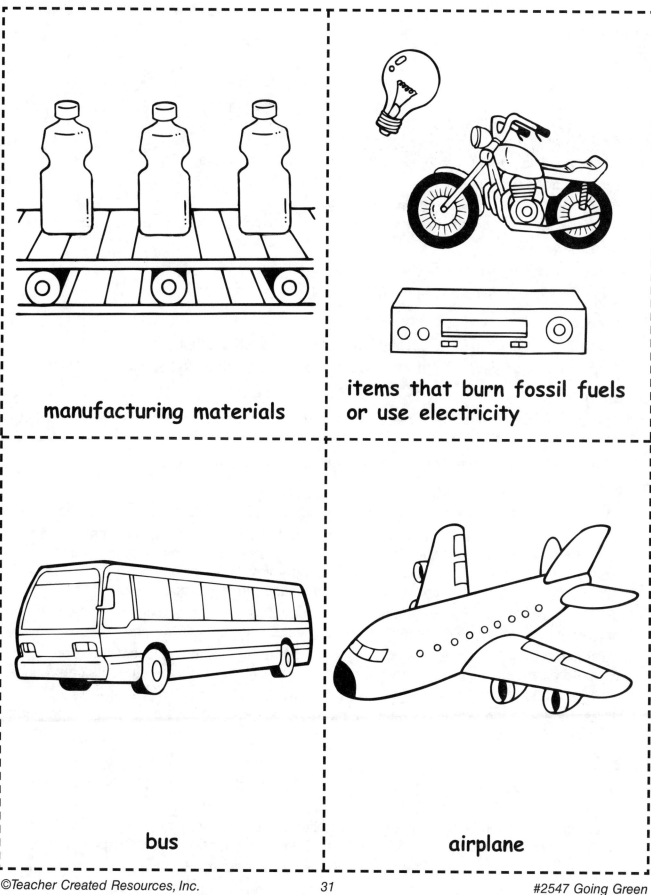

manufacturing materials

items that burn fossil fuels or use electricity

bus

airplane

Heal the Planet

Objective: Given information about activities related to "carbon footprints," the students will write prescriptions for a healthy planet.

Vocabulary

- atmosphere
- pollution

Materials

- Carbon Dioxide and Carbon Footprints explanations on page 29
- Prescription for a Healthy Planet on page 34
- Bandage Patterns on page 33 or bandages
  (eco-friendlier option: cloth rags cut in strips like bandages and permanent markers)
- tape or tacks
- copy of world map for display
- age-appropriate research materials (optional)

Preparation

1. Copy the Prescription for a Healthy Planet form for each student.
2. Copy a bandage pattern for each student or collect bandages to use for the activity.

Opening

1. Review the meaning of *fossil fuel, carbon dioxide*, and *carbon footprint* from the previous lesson as needed.
2. Have the students write three questions they have about carbon footprints.

Part 1

1. Review with the students the concept of carbon dioxide and its effect on the atmosphere.
2. Ask the students to recall what they have learned about ways in which excess carbon dioxide enters the *atmosphere* (the mixture of gases that surrounds a planet; air) to disrupt the natural balance. Discuss how carbon dioxide emissions create *pollution* (environmental contamination with man-made waste) in the atmosphere.
3. Pair each student with a partner. Have the students exchange questions. Instruct the students to write answers to their partner's questions and discuss them.
4. Ask students at random to share questions and answers to begin class discussion. Expand on the student responses as needed to talk about ways the students can reduce their carbon footprints.
5. Determine what additional research might be done and provide time and age-appropriate materials for student use.

Part 2

1. Explain that reducing the carbon footprint can help heal the planet. It's also good for us to live in a healthy environment.
2. Distribute to the students copies of Prescription for a Healthy Planet. Have each student write a prescription. They should write something they can do to help the planet.
3. Have the students write their remedies on bandages and attach them to a world map.

32

Heal the Planet *(cont.)*

Closing

1. Review the definitions of *atmosphere* and *pollution*.

2. Ask the students to share specific ways in which they have reduced their carbon footprint and helped heal the planet since beginning their study.

Extension

Encourage students to do some of the things discussed in class over the next two or three days to reduce their carbon footprints. Then have students write "get well cards" to planet Earth telling what they did to help heal the planet.

ELL Tip

Have the students illustrate their prescriptions for the planet on a separate sheet of paper, highlighting actions they can take to heal the planet (e.g., walking to school, reading a book, drinking from a refillable cup).

Bandage Patterns

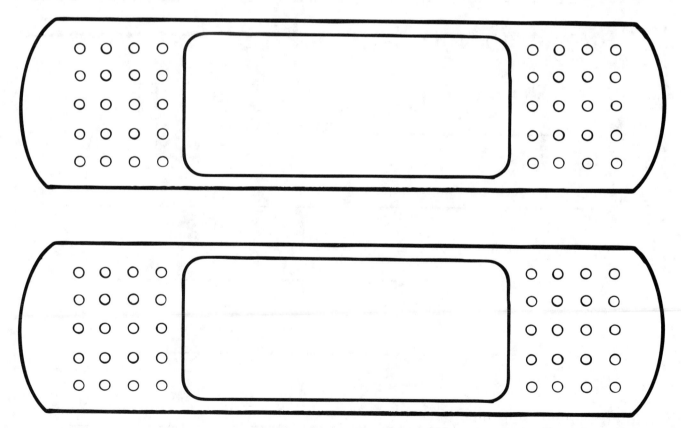

Prescription for a Healthy Planet

R
X

Date: _____

I will _____

_____

_____

Signature: _____

Prescription for a Healthy Planet

R
X

Date: _____

I will _____

_____

_____

Signature: _____

Energy Efficiency

Objective: Given information about the amount of energy electrical appliances use, the students will discover electricity requirements for specific devices in the classroom and create a graph to show which devices use the most electricity.

Vocabulary

- watt
- kilowatt hour

Materials

- Energy Consumption Form on page 37
- Energy Consumption Line Graph on page 36
- overhead projector, chart paper, or interactive whiteboard
- sheet of white paper for each student (eco-friendlier option: use individual student whiteboards and appropriate markers)
- index cards (optional)
- magazine pictures of electrical devices commonly found in a classroom (optional)

Preparation

1. Prepare an index card for each electrical device in the classroom indicating how much electricity (how many watts) each uses. Many appliances have a label indicating how many watts they use. Post the cards next to each device.

2. Review the sample Energy Consumption chart on page 37. It indicates average amounts of electricity used by common classroom or household items.

3. Copy the line graph onto a transparency or scan into an interactive whiteboard.

Opening

1. Introduce the basic unit of measurement used to measure electricity. Tell students that electricity is measured in *watts*. One thousand watts of energy used for one hour equals one *kilowatt hour* (kwh).

2. Draw this equation on the board to illustrate: **1,000 watts of energy for 1 hour = 1 kwh.**

Part 1

1. Have the students use a white sheet of paper or an individual whiteboard. Ask them to draw a line down the middle to create two columns. They will label one column "Item" and the other "Watts."

2. As an example, show the class the plate on the side of an item, such as the overhead projector that states how many watts the device uses. Refer the students to a sample index card posted next to an electrical device.

3. Have the students explore the room and list each appliance and the watts or electricity each uses.

4. Direct the students to write the name of the device in one column and the wattage in the other.

5. Have the students rank electrical devices in the order of electricity used.

Item	Watts
computer	150-340
light bulb	60

Energy Efficiency *(cont.)*

Part 2

1. Display the Energy Consumption Line Graph (based on the chart on page 37) on the overhead or whiteboard.

2. Have the students create a similar line graph and chart that lists the electrical devices in your classroom. The students will complete the graph to show the amount of energy various electrical devices use.

3. Challenge the students to add other items and information.

Closing

1. Review the vocabulary words, *watt*(s) and *kilowatt hour*(s), by playing a game of I Spy or a similar guessing game.

2. Use spatial and visual clues to have the students guess electrical devices in the room that use the most electricity or a certain number of watts or kilowatt hours.

Extensions

1. Conduct a discussion about how the class can save electricity. Here are some suggestions:

   • Turn off computers when not in use for extended periods of time (when the teacher is working directly with the students, out of the room for P.E., or at night).

   • Unplug dormant devices, such as televisions, when not in use.

   • Replace regular light bulbs with compact flourescent bulbs.

2. Ask the students to estimate how much electricity each suggestion would save. The students can figure the amount of watts per hour using the information from the lesson. Help them determine how much electricity would not be used during the hours the device is turned off.

ELL Tip

Direct the students to include pictures (drawn or cut from magazines) of each device when creating their line graph. Help with labeling as needed.

Energy Consumption Line Graph

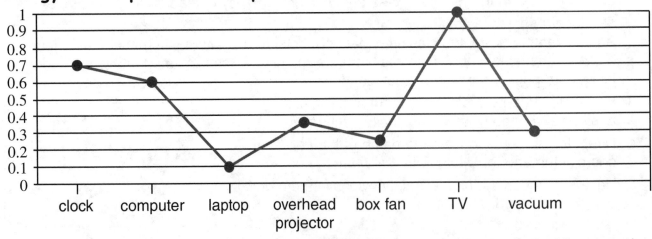

Energy Consumption

The amount of energy a device actually uses varies. The wattage listed on the label indicates the highest amount of electricity the device would use. A sample list is provided below.

1,000 watts of energy for 1 hour = 1 kilowatt hour (kwh)

Item	Watts	Hours	Kilowatt hours (kwh)
clock	3 watts	24 hours	.72 kwh
desktop computer	300 watts	2 hours	.6 kwh
laptop computer	100 watts approx.	2 hours	.1 kwh
overhead projector lamp	360 watts	1 hour	.36 kwh
box fan	125 watts	2 hours	.25 kwh
TV	100–300 watts	4 hours	approx. 1kwh
vacuum cleaner	600 watts	½ hour	.3 kwh

Energy Consumption Form

Item	Watts	Hours	Kilowatt hours (kwh)

Why Reduce Garbage?

Objective: Given an interactive, read-aloud experience, the students will participate and respond by suggesting alternate choices.

Vocabulary

- biodegradable
- break down / breakdown
- decompose
- landfill

Materials

- Healthy Environment vocabulary cards on page 40
- The "Breakdown on Landfills" story on page 41
- Biodegradable Breakdown Cards on pages 42–45
- overhead projector or interactive whiteboard and appropriate markers
- 3 sheets of cardstock for each pair of students

"Something is rotten."

Preparation

1. Read the story prior to sharing it with the students to become familiar with student sounds and actions.
2. Copy the Healthy Environment vocabulary cards and prepare them for use for a group presentation. Make additional copies as needed for student activities.
3. Copy the Biodegradable Breakdown Cards onto cardstock. Cut the cards apart to create game cards for each pair of students.

Opening

1. Refer to the Healthy Environment cards to write words and definitions randomly on the overhead or whiteboard.
2. Invite the students to match each word to its correct definition.
3. Explain that the students will learn how these words relate to keeping our environment healthy.

Part 1

1. Introduce hand motions and sound effects for the read-aloud story as indicated in "The Breakdown on Landfills" story.
2. Read the story aloud and model the hand motions.
3. Reread the story and have the students participate with hand motions at appropriate times in the story.

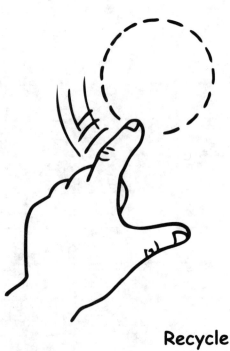

Recycle

38

 # Why Reduce Garbage? *(cont.)*

Part 2

1. Review "The Breakdown on Landfills" story. Remind the students that some items take longer to break down than others.

2. Pair each student with a partner. Tell the students that they are going to play a game similar to War.

   - Each pair will have a stack of game cards with estimated breakdowns.
   - Players should split the deck in half so each person has half the cards.
   - Each player turns over one card at a time.
   - The first player should read the card aloud, "A _____ takes at least _____ to break down."
   - The player whose card shows an item that breaks down faster than the other person's item takes both cards. If the breakdown times are the same, those cards are put in the "landfill," a pile in the middle that the players don't get to keep.
   - When the players have gone through their stack of cards, they take the cards they have "won" and play through the deck again.
   - Play continues until one player has captured all the cards.

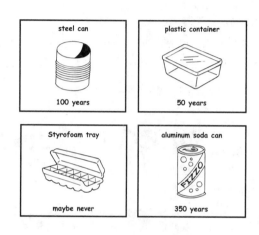

Closing

1. Ask the students what they can do with items that take a long time to biodegrade.
2. Have them suggest alternate ways to keep these items out of the landfill. (recycle, use things made from biodegradable materials, reuse, etc.)

Extension

If possible, arrange to take the class on a field trip to a landfill. Have the students view how trash is sorted and how much land is required for a landfill. Poll the students later for reactions and ideas for further reducing garbage.

ELL Tip

Slowly read the "The Breakdown on Landfills" story again with a small group. Consider recording the story for students to listen to again.

Ask the students to describe differences in trash: what they throw away, how they reduce trash, and how else they might use items they throw away. Encourage them to incorporate at least one vocabulary word (*decompose, landfill, biodegradable, break down, breakdown* into the discussion.)

Why Reduce Garbage? *(cont.)*

Healthy Environment

biodegradable	something that can be broken down naturally by bacteria
break down	v. to change something into smaller parts
breakdown	n. undergo a change or enter a new state
decompose	to rot or decay
landfill	garbage that is stacked and covered with earth

Why Reduce Garbage? *(cont.)*

The Breakdown on Landfills

A loud crash woke Lester with a start. He hated Monday—dumpster day. Lester nudged the piece of trash next to him. "Hey, what were the rumors we heard yesterday? Oh yeah, some workers are coming today to go through the trash. They want to know what people throw away."

"I remember now," Lester said. "They want to find out which trash breaks down the fastest. Many things here in the landfill do not break down."

The workers arrived carrying large garbage bags. They wore gloves. Carefully they began to sort through the trash.

"Look at this!" a man held up a glass bottle. "The label says 1913! This has been here a while."

"This banana peel sure is rotten. I almost slipped on it," his partner muttered. "It's probably been here only a week."

"Hey, look at this computer." The first man pointed to Lester. "How long do you think it will be here?"

"Unless someone recycles the computer, it will be here forever. I don't think computers rot."

The men sorting trash shook their heads. Lester heard them say, "Why do people throw so much stuff away?"

Hand Motions

trash or *garbage*—rub hands together as if crumpling a piece of paper

break down—pat hands on desk as if smashing down trash

landfill—one hand flat, other hand clapping on top as if filling a landfill

rotten or *rot*—hold hands to nose as if something stinks

recycles—draw a circle in the air with index finger

Why Reduce Garbage? (cont.)

Biodegradable Breakdown Cards

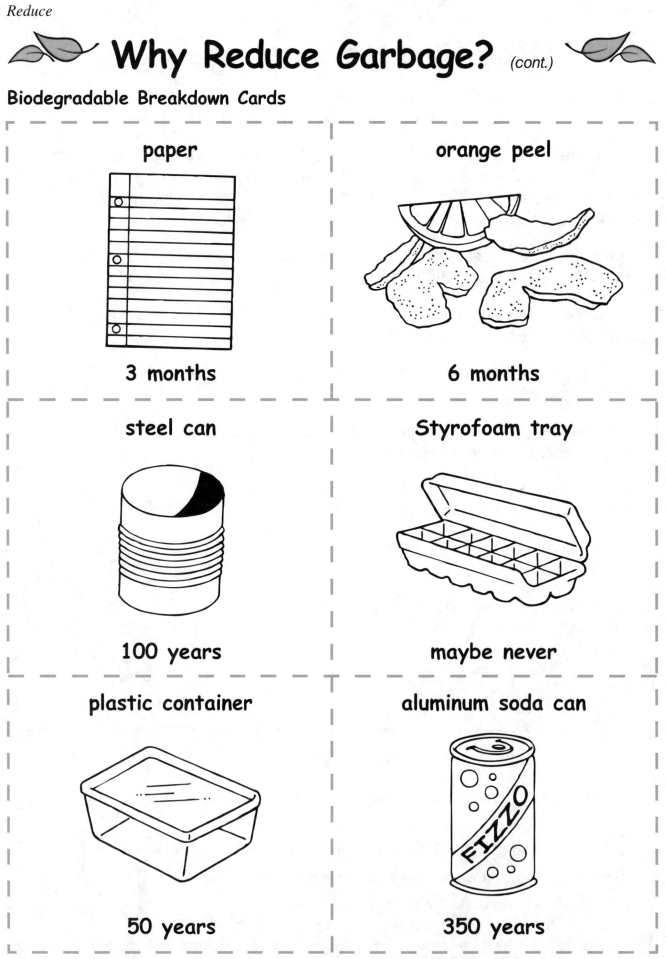

paper

3 months

orange peel

6 months

steel can

100 years

Styrofoam tray

maybe never

plastic container

50 years

aluminum soda can

350 years

42

Why Reduce Garbage? *(cont.)*

Biodegradable Breakdown Cards *(cont.)*

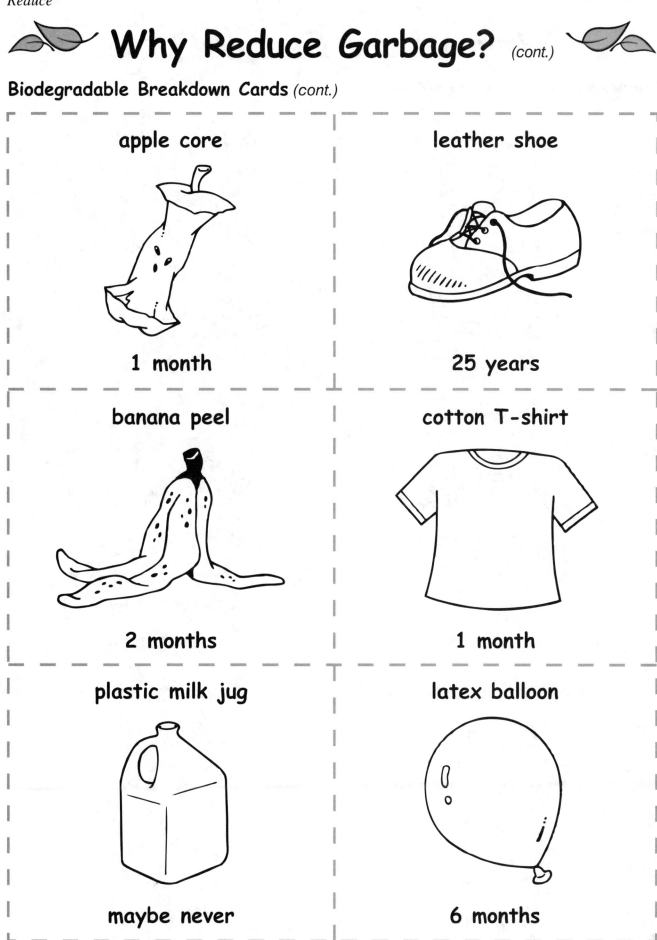

apple core

1 month

leather shoe

25 years

banana peel

2 months

cotton T-shirt

1 month

plastic milk jug

maybe never

latex balloon

6 months

Why Reduce Garbage? *(cont.)*

Biodegradable Breakdown Cards *(cont.)*

plastic garbage bag

10 years

wooden baseball bat

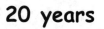

20 years

rope

3 months

wool sock

1 year

cardboard milk carton

MILK

5 years

nylon fabric

30 years

Why Reduce Garbage? *(cont.)*

Biodegradable Breakdown Cards *(cont.)*

car tire

maybe never

plastic six-pack ring

450 years

plastic water bottle

500 years

glass jar

maybe never

newspaper

GAZETTE

Read all about it!

2 weeks

plastic sandwich bags

400 years

Lunchtime Rhymes

Objective: Given a class-generated list of ideas, the students will create a chant, rap, or jingle to remind their classmates about environmentally friendly lunch practices.

Vocabulary

- reusable
- bulk

Materials

- Environmentally Friendly Lunch list on page 48
- overhead projector, chart paper, or interactive whiteboard and appropriate marker
- index card for each student (eco-friendlier option: individual student whiteboards, appropriate markers, and rags to erase)
- sample packaging from lunch items

Preparation

1. Copy the Environmentally Friendly Lunch list onto a transparency or scan into an interactive whiteboard for display.
2. Collect and clean typical packaging from student lunches.

Opening

1. Ask the students what they had for lunch. How was it packaged?
2. Review the concept that *packaging* is the wrapping, box, or container in which an item is placed or sold.
3. Ask the students to list what they threw away.
4. Ask if anything in their lunch was *reusable* (something that can be used again).

Part 1

1. Discuss the concept that an environmentally friendly lunch is one that has less packaging to throw away in a landfill.

2. Pose the question, "What are some ways you can help pack an environmentally friendly lunch?"

3. Allow the students two minutes to think about their answers to the question and have each student write his or her idea on an index card or an individual whiteboard.

4. Pair each student with a partner. Have them share the ideas they wrote.

5. Call on student pairs to report their ideas. Generate a class list on the projector or whiteboard, listing ways students can help pack an environmentally friendly lunch.

Lunchtime Rhymes (cont.)

Part 2

1. Discuss the concepts presented on the Environmentally Friendly Lunch list. Define terms such as *bulk* (to buy in large quantities; not in individual packages) if necessary.

2. If time permits, use the Vocabulary cards created in Environmental Perspectives (pages 14–17) to review words. Have the students add any new words to the set of cards.

3. Have student pairs create a chant, rap, or jingle to tell others how to pack a lunch that reduces waste.

Closing

1. Allow time for the students to present their jingles to the class.

2. Ask the students what they have learned about how lunch foods are packaged and reusable or bulk items that can be used in lunches.

Extension

Have the students create a "menu" for a student's lunch box using what they have learned. A school lunch might include a tuna sandwich in a reusable container, carrot sticks in a reusable container, and a few raisins purchased in bulk and put in a reusable container.

ELL Tip

During the Opening section of the lesson, show sample items in packaging (prepackaged snacks, fresh fruit in reusable plastic containers, etc.). Ask the students to explain which types of packaging are reusable.

Lunchtime Rhymes *(cont.)*

Environmentally Friendly Lunch

There are many ways to pack more environmentally friendly lunches. The way you shop, what you purchase, and how you package it all affect the end result.

- Help pack your lunch.

- Ask to use a refillable bottle for water or juice.

- Bring reusable silverware and wash it after each use.

- Ask to use a cloth napkin and remember to take it home and wash it.

- Offer to help put the bulk foods purchased into smaller containers.

- Help choose fresh fruits and vegetables you like to eat.

- Help read advertisements to find sales on local produce.

- Read food labels. If you cannot pronounce the ingredients, think twice about eating it.

- Resist marketing and advertising.

- Try to reduce the number of pre-packaged foods purchased.

- Consider packing homemade items (cookies, muffins, trail mix, applesauce) in reusable containers. Offer to help make these foods on the weekend and freeze them for use during the school week.

- Find grocery stores that have bakeries offering smaller quantities of baked items.

- Remind family members to bring cloth bags to the store on shopping days.

- Check with your school to see if your class can plant a garden to grow fresh produce.

In the Community

Objective: Given a role-play exercise, the students will observe ways they can reduce the amount of waste they throw away.

Vocabulary

- waste (noun)
- consume

Materials

- "Environmental Pie" script on page 51
- overhead projector, chart paper, or interactive whiteboard and appropriate marker
- piece of scrap paper for each student
- props for fast food scene (e.g., ketchup packets, straws, napkins, disposable Styrofoam containers)
- piece of poster board or cardstock for each student (optional)

Preparation

1. Make copies of the "Environmental Pie" script for three volunteers. Use actual student names, perhaps writing them in before making copies. Roles may be played by boys or girls.
2. Work with the student volunteers to practice the skit.

Opening

1. Review with the students the meaning of the word *disposable*. Tell the students that to *consume* an item is to use it up, and then dispose of the packaging.
2. Use the projector or whiteboard to generate a class list of the types of *waste* (garbage or something left over and not needed) that the students encounter in the community.

Part 1

1. Pose three questions to the students:
    - Where was the last place you went in our community?
    - What did you do while you were there?
    - What did you consume while you were there?
    - What waste did you create while there?

2. Have the students write their responses on pieces of scrap paper. If the students have trouble remembering what they threw away, suggest:
    - At a fast food restaurant, you may have thrown away disposable containers.
    - At a grocery store, you may have thrown away a gum wrapper.
    - After going to a department store, you may have thrown away a plastic bag.
    - You may have thrown away trash from the car.

3. Have the students share with partners what they threw away while they were in the community.

In the Community *(cont.)*

Part 2

1. Have the student volunteers present the skit, "Environmental Pie."

2. Conduct a class discussion about how participants in the demonstration reduced garbage.

   • They did not use plastic straws.

   • They took only what they needed of individual packets such as cheese, red peppers, or salt.

   • They ate at a restaurant that provided reusable plates and utensils if they ate their food there.

Part 3

Have the students create a personal chart similar to the one shown below.

Place	Trash	How I Can Reduce Trash
library	papers	recycle
video game store	plastic bags	decline a bag
grocery store	plastic bags	put groceries in reusable cloth bags
fast food restaurant	straws and wrappers	don't use a straw
sporting event	disposable cups	use a refillable water bottle

Closing

1. Expand the students' thinking by asking them to brainstorm ways they could reduce waste when they are away from home.

2. Have the students discuss how they can reduce their use of disposable items at home.

Extension

Obtain permission to work with a business in your community. Have the students make posters depicting ways members of the community can reduce trash when they visit that place. For example, many stores have posted signs on the doors reminding shoppers to use cloth bags. Students can make signs such as the following: "Please pick up trash!" "Recycle," and "Bring Your Own Bag!"

ELL Tip

Work with a small group to slowly reread the "Environmental Pie" skit. Have the students act out the skit as you read it aloud.

In the Community *(cont.)*

Environmental Pie

(Two kids and a parent enter a pizza restaurant. They stand, looking at the menu board.)

Kid 1: Dad (Mom), are we eating here or are we getting "take out"?

Parent: Let's eat here. We're not in a hurry.

Kid 2: Doesn't this restaurant have reusable plates, cups, and silverware? If it does, we won't create as much trash if we eat here. We learned about trash and litter at school today.

Parent: Okay, if you're ready, let's order. We'll have a medium pepperoni pizza.
(*They sit at a table and wait.*)

Parent: What else did you learn about trash? Maybe you could also pick up the trash in your room. (*smiles and laughs*)

Kid 1: We learned not to take extra things we don't really need, like salt or ketchup packets because they'll probably get thrown away.

Kid 2: They don't have salt or ketchup at a pizza place.

Parent: They do have cheese and red pepper in individual packets, though. While we're waiting, let's get our drinks.

Kid 2: Okay. I'm not going to take a straw because it's made of plastic and can't be recycled.

Kid 1: Me neither.

Parent: Oh, good. You won't blow the papers all over the table!

Kid 2: May we have some quarters for the games, then?

Parent: Maybe later. Looks like our pizza is almost ready.

Kid 1: Does anyone want Parmesan cheese or red pepper? I'll get some packets.

Kid 2: But only what we need, remember?

Kid 1: That's why I'm asking.

Kid 2: Yeah, I'd like one packet of red peppers, please.

Parent: We each need a napkin, too. Just a few—not a whole handful—they'll just get thrown away. (*They all settle down at the table and begin eating.*)

Kid 2: Yum! This is good!

Kid 1: And good for the environment, too!

New Ways of Thinking

Objective: Given a diagram, the students will learn to think through the process of refusing to use or purchase items that harm the environment.

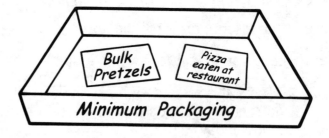

Vocabulary

- packaging
- excessive

Materials

- Just Say No sign on page 53
- Choosing Green on page 54
- Thinking Through the Process on page 55
- overhead projector, chart paper or interactive whiteboard, and appropriate markers
- 2″ x 3″ index card for each student (eco-friendlier option: heavy scrap paper)
- 4 shallow cardboard boxes
- 2 pieces of cardboard
- marker

Preparation

1. Enlarge the Just Say No sign for display.
2. Copy the Choosing Green diagram onto a transparency or scan it into an interactive whiteboard for display. Also copy the diagram for each student. (Make additional copies of the diagram if using the ELL Tip on page 53.)
3. Label two boxes *Excessive Packaging* and two boxes *Minimum Packaging*.
4. Label one piece of cardboard *Refuse* and one *Accept* to create two table signs.

Opening

1. Hold up the Just Say No sign. Ask the students what this means. (You will make a choice *not* to do something.)
2. Explain that whenever we choose to do one thing, we are actively making a choice *not* to do something else.
3. Review with the students the definition of the verb *refuse* (ri-fyooz) in the context of this discussion. (To say you will not do something or accept something. Explain that this word has the idea of rejecting something because you do not want to use it or you believe this is not the right thing to do.)
4. Have the students explain what *packaging* is. (the wrapping, box, or container in which an item is sold)
5. Briefly introduce the concept of *excessive* packaging. Tell the students that an item has too much packaging if it has the following:
   - layers of plastic
   - plastic foam
   - individual wrapping inside larger wrapped packaging
6. Tell the students that the concept of minimum packaging means the opposite of excessive packaging.

 # New Ways of Thinking *(cont.)*

Part 1

1. Display the Choosing Green diagram on the overhead or whiteboard. Enlist the students' participation as you talk through the decision-making process.
2. Share with the students the first example from Thinking Through the Process.

Part 2

1. Distribute the index cards to the students. Have the students list on the card one item they recently purchased.
2. Distribute the student copies of Choosing Green. Have the students use a highlighter to trace their thinking for the item they purchased. The students should trace their thoughts as if they were purchasing the item today with new information about packaging.
3. Share with the students the second example from Thinking Through the Process to help them think through their purchases, if necessary.

Closing

1. Set up two table areas. Place the **Refuse** sign on one table and the **Accept** sign on the other table. Place one box labeled "Excessive Packaging" and one box labeled "Minimum Packaging" on each table.
2. Review the signs and labels on the boxes with the class. Have students tell what each sign or label means.
3. Call on student volunteers to place their index cards in the appropriate box and tell in what way the packaging was excessive or minimal. Have them state why they would choose to accept or refuse to purchase the item.

Extension

Have the students write a letter to the manufacturer telling why they would or would not choose to buy this item in the future, based on its type of packaging.

ELL Tip

Talk through the Choosing Green diagram with a small group of students. Use an example of a product and ask the students each question in the process. Have them use a highlighter on a clean copy of the diagram to follow the process of thinking.

Just Say No

New Ways of Thinking (cont.)

— Choosing Green —

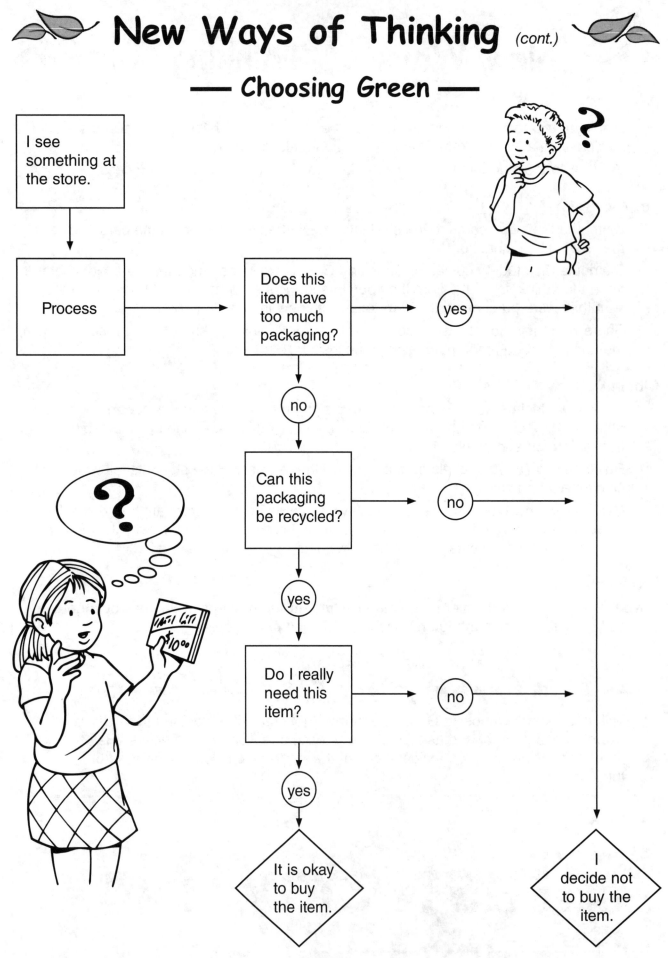

I see something at the store.

↓

Process → Does this item have too much packaging? → yes →

no ↓

Can this packaging be recycled? → no →

yes ↓

Do I really need this item? → no →

yes ↓

It is okay to buy the item.

I decide not to buy the item.

New Ways of Thinking *(cont.)*

Thinking Through the Process—Example 1

I want to get some new tennis shoes, but I'm not sure if it's a good idea. When I go shopping with a grownup, I'll ask myself these questions to help me decide what to do.

- **Do these shoes have minimum packaging?** Yes, they come in a box without any extra plastic or wrapping.

- **Can the packaging be recycled or reused?** Yes, I can break down the box and recycle it with mixed paper. Or I can use the box for storage or to wrap a gift.

- **Do I really need the shoes?** I'll look at the pair I have to see if I can still wear them for a while. They look okay. I'll wait and get new shoes later when I need them. Even though I can answer two of these questions "yes," because I do not really need this item, I'll decide not to buy it.

Thinking Through the Process—Example 2

I want to buy a new DVD with the allowance and birthday money I have saved up. It's in a plastic case, shrink wrapped in plastic, and has a plastic key device so someone cannot steal it. I ask myself these three questions.

- **Does this DVD have minimum packaging?** This item does have excessive packaging, so my answer is "No, it does not have minimum packaging." I might be able to find a DVD at another store that has minimum packaging without quite so many layers of plastic.

- **Can the packaging be recycled?** Plastic wrapping like this cannot be recycled, so I have to go to the "No" connector for the second question.

- **Do I really need the DVD?** I do not really need this. At this point, I have options. I can go to a friend's house and watch the movie with my friend, buy it used with less packaging, rent it, or save my money for when I need something more important.

Excessive Packaging

Objective: Given a review of the features present in excessive packaging, the students will identify and display examples of excessive and minimal packaging.

Vocabulary
- disposable
- refillable

Materials
- sample newspaper or magazine advertisements
- 12" x 18" sheet of white paper for each group
- colored pencils, crayons, or markers
- scissors

Preparation
1. Have the students bring in newspaper or magazine advertisements for a few days prior to the lesson.

Opening
1. Discuss with the students the words *disposable* (made to be thrown away after use) and *refillable* (can be refilled again and again) by asking the students in which other contexts they have heard these words used before (previous lessons, environmental concerns, in the context of shopping during the holidays).
2. Clarify the definitions as necessary.
3. Tell the students that they will explore advertising to learn more about how the products we buy are packaged.

Part 1
1. Review the features that indicate a product has too much packaging:
   - has layers of plastic
   - has plastic foam
   - is in an individually wrapped package inside a larger wrapped package
   - has multiple layers—paper, foil, plastic, cardboard (e.g., bag and box [cereal]; bottle and box [vitamins]; plastic, bubble wrap, hard plastic case, possibly box [CD]).

2. Divide the students into groups of three to five students.
3. Instruct them to use magazine or newspaper advertisements to find and identify examples of excessive and non-excessive packaging. Have the students cut out pictures of each.

Excessive Packaging (cont.)

Part 2

1. Each group will use a large sheet of white paper and fold it in half widthwise.

2. Have the students label one side of the paper "Excessive" and the other half of the paper "Minimum."

3. Direct the students to place the pictures they cut out in the appropriate column on their pages.

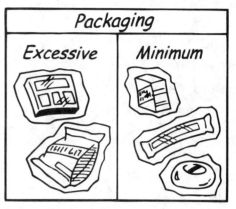

Closing

1. Have the students write descriptive sentences to tell why they placed specific items in each column. For example, this snack food advertisement shows a picture of a bag. It looks like the bag has paper on the outside and is lined with foil. This is excessive packaging because it has more than one layer, and the packaging cannot be easily recycled.

2. Encourage the students to use vocabulary words appropriately as they write their descriptions.

3. Add the descriptions to the 2-column miniposters.

4. Display the finished products. Allow time for viewing and discussion. If appropriate, pose the question, "Why might there be excessive packaging?"

    Possible reasons for excessive packaging might include the following:

    Safety—sharp items; medicines

    Theft prevention—electronics; high-priced items

    Marketing—more eye-catching or takes up more room on the shelf

Extension

Invite the students to be part of the solution for the problem of excessive packaging. Challenge them to design new packages for items that use non-recyclable packaging or too much packaging. Examples might include scissors, glue sticks, or CDs.

ELL Tip

Apply vocabulary words in a familiar context to help the students understand the meanings.

- Felipe eats an *excessive* amount of sugar.
- I had a hard time opening the plastic *packaging* on my new CD.
- They used *disposable* paper plates at the picnic and then threw them away.
- Some plastic water bottles are *refillable*.

 # Avoid Plastic

Objective: Given information to read, students will share their learning with classmates and create a class summary about how people can avoid using too much plastic.

Vocabulary

- plastic
- natural gas
- petroleum
- crude oil
- nonrenewable

Materials

- Why Should People Avoid Plastic? article on page 60 (*Reading Level 5.0*)
- Why Do We Use Plastic? article on page 61 (*Reading Level 2.9*)
- How Can We Use Less Plastic? article on page 62 (*Reading Level 4.3*)
- interactive whiteboard or overhead projector and appropriate markers
- sheet of white drawing paper for each student
- colored pencils, crayons, or markers
- Glossary on pages 93–96

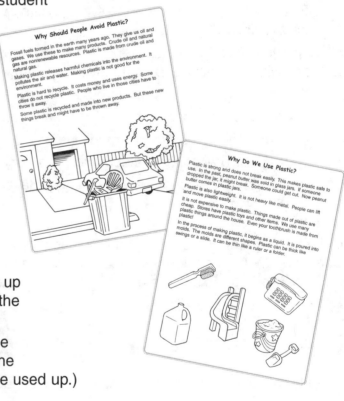

Preparation

1. Make copies of the articles as needed for student groups.
2. Consider grouping the students based on the reading level of each article.

Opening

1. Introduce the vocabulary by asking the students to define the following words: *plastic, natural gas, nonrenewable, crude oil,* and *petroleum.*
2. Confirm the class definitions by looking up the words in a dictionary or by sharing the glossary definitions.
3. Help the students identify and define the prefix in *nonrenewable* as they define the word. (A nonrenewable resource can be used up.)

Part 1

1. Divide the students into six groups, based on reading ability. (Two groups will read the same article.)
2. If you do not have students who are able to read the highest level selection, read it aloud to the class and have the groups discuss and summarize the content as part of their group discussion.

Avoid Plastic *(cont.)*

Part 2

1. Conduct a "jigsaw" activity. After the groups have finished reading their selections, have at least one student from each group rotate to another group to share the information they read in their first group.

2. Continue rotating until students have read or heard a summary of each of the three articles.

3. Call the students back together. Use an overhead or whiteboard to create a class summary about why and how people can avoid using too much plastic.

Closing

1. Ask the students what they noticed about the use of the vocabulary words in the reading selections. Did the words define other words, explain concepts, or describe how something looks or acts?

2. Use student responses to clarify the vocabulary as needed.

Extension

Have the students use drawing paper and colored pencils or other media to create a cartoon about using less plastic. Remind the students that cartoons have pictures and words, usually with dialogue, and the pictures should show action. Allow time for the students to share their cartoons with the class or provide an area where the drawings can be displayed.

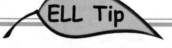

ELL Tip

Work with a small group to read the Why Do We Use Plastic? article. Scaffold the students by having them participate in echo or choral reading.

Avoid Plastic *(cont.)*

Why Should People Avoid Plastic?

Fossil fuels formed in the earth many years ago. They give us oil and gases. We use these to make many products. Crude oil and natural gas are nonrenewable resources. Plastic is made from crude oil and natural gas.

Making plastic releases harmful chemicals into the environment. It pollutes the air and water. Making plastic is not good for the environment.

Plastic is hard to recycle. It costs money and uses energy. Some cities do not recycle plastic. People who live in those cities have to throw it away.

Some plastic is recycled and made into new products. But these new things break and might have to be thrown away.

Avoid Plastic *(cont.)*

Why Do We Use Plastic?

Plastic is strong and does not break easily. This makes plastic safe to use. In the past, peanut butter was sold in glass jars. If someone dropped the jar, it might break. Someone could get cut. Now peanut butter comes in plastic jars.

Plastic is also lightweight. It is not heavy like metal. People can lift and move plastic easily.

It is not expensive to make plastic. Things made out of plastic are cheap. Stores have plastic toys and other items. We use many plastic things around the house. Even your toothbrush is made from plastic!

A plastic product begins as a liquid. The liquid is poured into molds. The molds are different shapes. Plastic can be thick like swings or a slide. It can be thin like a ruler or a folder.

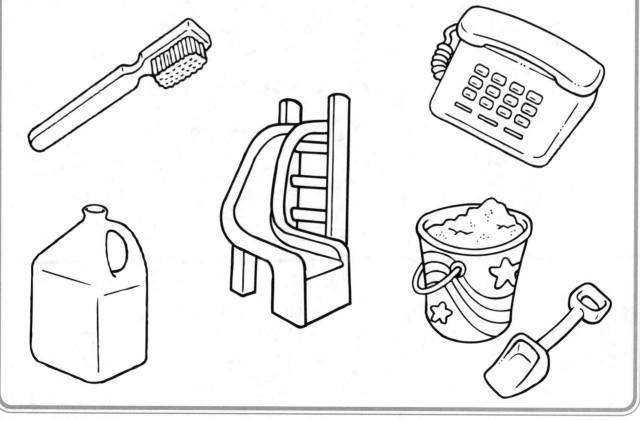

Avoid Plastic *(cont.)*

How Can We Use Less Plastic?

People can choose reusable containers. The same container can be used again. People can buy food or other things in bulk and put them in their own boxes, containers, or jars.

A person can buy one large bottle of soap instead of many small bottles of soap. Glue also comes in large bottles. It can be put in smaller bottles.

People can take cloth bags to the store instead of using paper or plastic bags. Look for packaging that can be recycled. For example, some toys are in a plastic case. Others come in cardboard boxes. People can make a choice to buy products that do not have too much plastic packaging.

62

Trash to Treasure

Objective: Given examples and the opportunity to brainstorm ideas, the students will describe how to make something new from trash.

Vocabulary

- repurpose
- durable
- STOP

Materials

- index card for each student (eco-friendlier option: heavy scrap paper)
- clean "trash" items (e.g., broken pencil, margarine tub, pie tin, individual-sized applesauce container)

Preparation

1. Gather a variety of clean trash items for a class display.

Opening

1. Introduce to the students the acronym *STOP*. Tell them that each time they are about to throw something away, they should first think of the letters in STOP: Stop, Think, Options, Participate. In other words, they should . . .

     1) **Stop**

     2) **Think** about the "trash" item

     3) decide if throwing away the item is the best **option**, and finally

     4) make the decision that allows them to **participate** in helping the environment.

2. Introduce the word *repurpose*. Show examples of things that have been repurposed, or used in a new way. Talk with the students about why it is important for an item to be *durable* (strong enough to be reused) if you would like to repurpose it.

     - An egg carton can hold small breakable items such as seashells.

     - Holes can be added to the bottom of a plastic margarine tub for drainage so it can be used to grow a plant.

     - A cleaned cloth napkin with stains can be reused as a cleaning rag.

Part 1

1. Remind the students that any time they throw something away, they should stop and consider the options for how they could reuse the item.

2. Give each student an index card. Have the students write one thing they have reused and how they have used it in a new or different way.

3. Direct the students to gather with classmates who reused similar objects. Have the students share their ideas and make associations to think of new uses for the items.

Trash to Treasure *(cont.)*

Part 2

1. Gather the students as a class again. Provide three clean "trash" items that could be reused and challenge the groups of students to brainstorm a list of new uses.

2. Have the students brainstorm and think creatively to give examples of how each item could be reused. For instance, a broken pencil can be used as a label to identify vegetables grown in a container.

3. Post the lists and continue to add to them.

4. At the end of a set amount of time, discuss with the students which item could be reused in the most ways, most creatively, or most efficiently (i.e., using all parts of the reused item).

5. Divide the students into groups and have them make some of the creations they suggested.

Closing

1. Have the students write a descriptive paragraph or directions for how to repurpose an item—to make something new from a piece of trash.

2. Challenge the students to use a different item from one already discussed in class.

Extension

Have the students go on a scavenger hunt—around the school, at home, in the classroom or library—to find and list items that could be reused (e.g., scrap paper, empty glue bottle, aluminum soda can). Have them write one possible new use for the item. If desired, compile student suggestions into a small class flyer for distribution to others around the school.

ELL Tip

Allow the students to draw pictures to show how they reused items when they share with their group.

The Buzz on Batteries

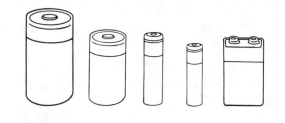

Objective: Given samples, the students will distinguish between rechargeable and non-rechargeable batteries and understand why we use rechargeable batteries.

Vocabulary

- chemical
- hazardous
- rechargeable

Materials

- Battery Picture Cards on page 67
- overhead projector, chart paper or interactive whiteboard, and appropriate markers
- empty packaging from a variety of batteries
- battery pictures from the Internet, magazines, or newspaper advertisements (variety of batteries, including a car battery and camera battery)
- samples of actual batteries (e.g., 9 volt from smoke detector, calculator battery, laptop computer battery, flashlight batteries, battery from a remote control)
- sheet of writing paper for each student
  (eco-friendlier option: use individual student whiteboards and appropriate markers)
- ten 2" x 3" cards

Preparation

1. Number the cards to correspond to battery samples or pictures. Provide no more than 10 cards even if you have more than 10 samples.

Opening

1. Engage the students in a discussion about things they use that require batteries (e.g., toys, toothbrushes, remote controls, small lights or clocks, MP3 player). Generate a list on the overhead or whiteboard.
2. Expand the list to include items students may not personally use (car, calculator, smoke detector, camera).
3. Explain that batteries contain *chemicals*, substances that interact with each other, in this case to make electricity. These chemicals are *hazardous*, or dangerous.
4. Tell the students that some batteries are rechargeable and some are not. Ask the students what *rechargeable* means. (You can charge the battery and use it again instead of throwing away the battery.)

Part 1

1. Ask the students why someone might want to use a rechargeable battery. (It saves money; you do not have to buy new batteries often; you do not need to throw old batteries away; it is better for the environment.)
2. Explain that some batteries charge as they are used. For example, a car battery recharges when the engine is running, and a computer battery recharges when the computer is plugged in. Some batteries cannot be recharged, such as those in some toothbrushes, flashlights, and medical items.
3. Introduce the concept that many items take either non-rechargeable batteries or rechargeable batteries, such as many toys and hand-held devices.

 # The Buzz on Batteries *(cont.)*

Part 2

1. Display the Battery Picture Cards.
2. Have the students identify the picture of a rechargeable battery.
3. Point out words one would see on a rechargeable battery. These words and symbols indicate the battery can be recharged:
   - nickel metal-hydride (NiMH)
   - nickel cadmium (NiCD)
   - nickel zinc (NiZN)
   - Lithium Ion
   - rechargeable

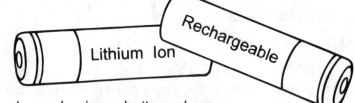

4. Explain that rechargeable batteries are charged using a battery charger that plugs into an electrical outlet. It takes electricity to recharge batteries.

Part 3

1. Instruct the students to sort the batteries (or packages) into chargeable and non-rechargeable batteries.
2. Have the students consider why it might be a good idea to recharge batteries. Ask them what happens to batteries you cannot recharge. (They are thrown away.)
3. Explain that batteries cannot just be thrown away. Not only do batteries take up space in a landfill, but they contain hazardous chemicals and must be disposed of properly so they do not harm the environment.
4. Distribute battery samples and battery-related pictures among the students.
5. Have the students investigate and explore the batteries (or packages) to become familiar with labels and different types of batteries.

Closing

1. Collect the battery samples and pictures. Review with the students the key terms: *chemical*, *hazardous*, and *rechargeable*.
2. Give each student a sheet of writing paper. Have the students number their paper from 1 to 10, based on the number of items on which you plan to quiz the students.
3. Hold up one battery sample and a number card, beginning with the number 1. Ask the students to write "yes" or "no" to indicate whether or not that type of battery is rechargeable.
4. After the students have completed the quiz, have them swap papers. Go over the correct responses. The students may draw smiley faces next to any correct answers.

Extension

Have the students write one or two sentences about how using rechargeable batteries helps the environment.

 ELL Tip

For the Extension activity, provide sentence frames as needed for the students.

- You save _____ when you use rechargeable batteries.
- You do not _____ when you use rechargeable batteries.

The Buzz on Batteries (cont.)

Battery Picture Cards

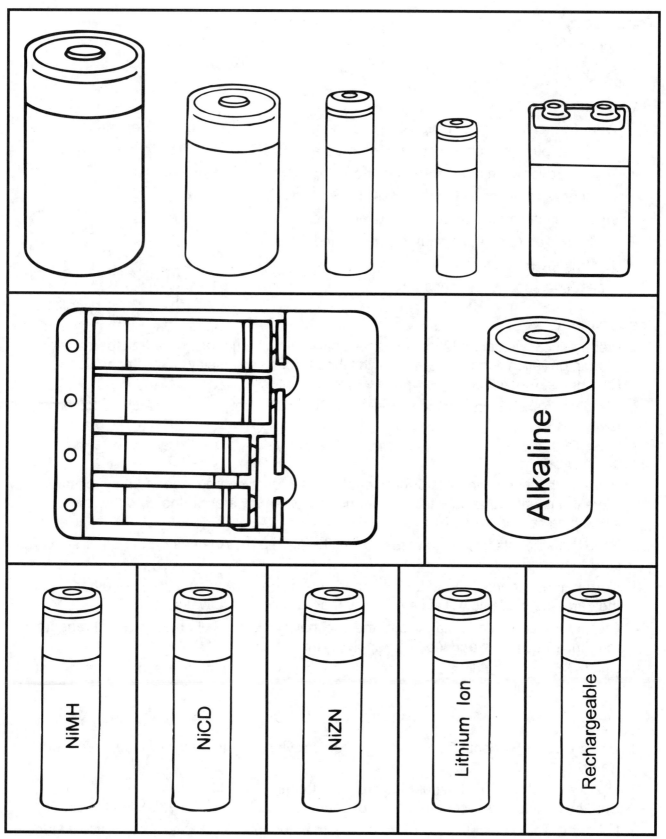

Alkaline

NiMH

NiCD

NiZN

Lithium Ion

Rechargeable

Precious Rainwater

Objective: Given a class discussion about where water comes from and how people use water, the students will make a rain catcher to collect rainwater for various uses.

Vocabulary

- conserve
- source

Materials

- What Students Can Do miniposter on page 22 from the How to Go Green lesson
- overhead projector, chart paper or interactive whiteboard, and appropriate markers
- index card for each student (eco-friendlier option: heavy scrap paper)
- weather report information from newspaper, radio, or Internet
- empty, reusable containers (e.g., coffee cans, household containers)
- craft supplies (e.g., paint, markers, odds and ends)
- Technology Resources on page 91.
- measuring spoons and cups (optional)

Preparation

1. Prepare local weather information, specifically rainfall amounts, on a transparency or scan information into an interactive whiteboard for class display. (See Technology Resources, Reuse section, on page 91.)
2. Identify a place on campus in which the students can set their rain catchers to collect rainwater.

Opening

1. Have each student write his or her name in the corner on one side of an index card. Have them write what they think it means to *conserve* water on the card. (to save something from loss or waste)
2. Have the students exchange cards. Have them write their names on the other side of the card they received.
3. Instruct the students to read their partner's definition of *conserve*. On the other side of the card, the students will write one way they can conserve water.
4. Check for student understanding of the vocabulary word. Call on students at random to read their definitions and ideas for applying this concept.
5. Use the students' understanding of water to review the meaning of *source* in this context. (source of a supply)

Part 1

1. Use the What Students Can Do miniposter to review why it is a good idea to conserve water.
2. Use the overhead or whiteboard to create a T-chart. Label the left column, "Water Sources." As a class, generate a list of sources of water. (oceans, lakes, rivers, rain)
3. Label the right column, "Water Uses." Ask the students to list ways people use water.

68

Precious Rainwater (cont.)

Part 1 (cont.)

4. Invite the students to match water sources with water uses. For example, people use water from a river or stream to water crops and grow food. People acquire drinking water from ground sources, such as groundwater and aquifers; precipitation (e.g., rain, hail, snow, fog); surface water, such as rivers, streams, glaciers; and the sea through desalination.

5. Display the local weather information on the overhead or whiteboard. Discuss with the students the amount of rain that falls. Is it above or below average for the time of year?

6. Point out that much of our water usage does not require clean tap water. Ask the students to identify water uses for which rainwater could potentially be used. (watering plants, bathing a dog, rinsing outdoor items such as muddy boots)

Part 2

1. Refer to the rainwater discussion in Part 1 to clarify and add to the list of potential uses for rainwater.

2. Explain that the students will make a rain catcher. This will be a container in which they can collect rainwater to use as an alternative to using tap water.

3. Provide cans and plastic containers for the students to create rain catchers. Have the students decorate their containers.

4. Direct the students to place their rain catchers in the prearranged place to collect rainfall.

5. Check and record rainfall periodically and discuss collection amounts. If no rain falls, discuss those implications.

Closing

Have the students write sentences to answer the following reflective questions.

- How does collecting rainwater help us conserve water?
- Why is it important to conserve water?
- For what purposes can we use rainwater?
- What happens when it does not rain?
- What can people in drought areas do?

rainwater

Extension

Have the students measure and record the amount of rainwater that falls in a given period of time. Direct them to measure and record the amount of water they use for everyday tasks such as watering a garden, rinsing off muddy shoes, or filling a bucket with water. Ask the students to compare the amounts and estimate how much water they can conserve by collecting rainwater.

ELL Tip

Provide sentence frames for the students to help them answer the Closing activity questions.

If we collect and use rainwater, we conserve water because _____.

It is important to conserve water because _____.

We can use rainwater to _____.

During a drought, people can _____.

What Is Recycling?

Objective: Given pictures, the students will categorize items into those that can be recycled and those that cannot be recycled and will draw a scene correctly depicting recyclable materials.

Vocabulary
- cycle
- closing the loop
- process

Materials
- Recycling Resources on page 72
- Becoming G-R-R-R-R-R-R-EEN—Learn the Rs on pages 20–21
- pictures of different items that can be recycled
- 6 empty containers for each group
- sheet of drawing paper for each student
- appropriately colored pencils, crayons, or markers

Preparation
1. Read Recycling Resources to become familiar with the types of materials that can be recycled.
2. Have the students bring in pictures from a variety of sources such as magazines, advertisements, the Internet, etc., showing different items that can be recycled.
3. Have the students label one set of containers for each group. Use the following labels: paper, glass, metal, plastic, cardboard, and wood.
4. If using the ELL Tip, direct the students to collect pictures of glass windows, wood, rocks or gravel, bricks, etc., to illustrate the sample scenario in Part 3.

Opening
1. Work with the students to break the word *recycle* into parts to deepen students' comprehension of the word and concept.
2. Explain that *re-* means to do something again. The root word, *cycle*, refers to a series of steps that is done over and over again. When something is recycled it goes through the process again. Paper is recycled to make other paper products. Glass is reheated and formed into a new shape so that people can use the glass again. Scrap metal is compacted and reprocessed into steel. When an item is recycled, it has not gone out of the loop into the landfill. This is referred to as *closing the loop*.
3. Discuss the definition of the word *process* as necessary. (an organized series of steps or actions that produce a particular result)

Part 1
1. Review with the students why recycling is a good idea.
2. Have the students use their knowledge of the word *conserve* from the Precious Rainwater lesson to tell what it means to conserve natural resources.
3. Use Becoming G-R-R-R-R-R-R-EEN—Learn The Rs to discuss how recycling can help conserve resources.
   - Recycling uses less energy.
   - Since we get some energy from nonrenewable fossil fuels, recycling saves those valuable resources.
   - Recycling does not use new materials, which conserves natural resources, such as trees and ore from the earth.

What Is Recycling? *(cont.)*

Part 1 *(cont.)*

4. As a class, generate a list of materials that can be recycled. Refer to Recycling Resources as necessary. Add to the list. Encourage the students to think of substances that come from nature, such as wood (paper), glass, or metal. Tell the students that some communities have the technology to recycle plastic, but not all do.
5. Explain that items that cannot be recycled include things made from mixed materials, such as juice boxes, squeezable bottles, and ink pens. These things go into landfills.

Part 2

1. Divide students into groups. Make sure each group has a set of labeled containers.
2. Students sort their pictures into the appropriate recycling "bins."
3. Call on the students to share where they placed an item and why.

Part 3

1. Distribute drawing paper. Tell the students you will describe a sample scenario.
2. Ask students to sketch the scene described and add items that can be recycled.
3. Read the following sample scenario aloud to the class.

   The school district plans to tear down Crumble School. Before they tear down the school, they will build a new school in the fields behind the existing school. Once the new school is complete, the bulldozer comes in with other equipment and they begin to dismantle the old school. Draw a picture to show the piles they made of recyclable materials from the old school. (glass from windows, bricks from walls, wood from trim, rock from parking lot, asphalt, or other gravel)

Closing

1. Have the students select one "pile" from their drawing. They should sketch the recycle symbol. Have them show how that material could be recycled, or go through a process to make another product of that same material. For example, the students could select the rock, write or draw the rock next to the first arrow in the symbol, write or draw crushed rock next to the second arrow in the symbol, and write or draw a road for the third arrow in the symbol.

2. Remind the students that if they cannot recycle something, they should try to find a way to reuse the item.
3. Have the students share their recycling symbol drawings and their thoughts.

Reread the scenario from Part 3 with a small group. Show corresponding pictures collected to illustrate the scene as you read.

What Is Recycling? (cont.)

Recycling Resources

Paper

magazines

mail

phone books

computer paper

binder paper

construction paper

brown paper bags

catalogs

paperboard (cereal boxes, etc.)

Newspaper

newspapers

circulars

Cardboard

boxes

packaging

Glass

bottles

jars

Plastic

water bottles

soda bottles

juice bottles

food containers

Ferrous Metal (magnetic, containing iron)

steel framing

Non-ferrous Metal

aluminum cans

aerosol cans
(check requirements of local facility)

aluminum foil (clean, no food)

metal clothes hangers

tin cans

TV dinner trays

pie plates

72

Hunt for the Green

Objective: Given instruction on recyclable materials, the students will correctly identify and label recyclable and non-recyclable items in the classroom.

Vocabulary
- recyclable
- synthetic

Materials
- Recycling chart on page 75
- Recycling Symbols on pages 25–26 from the Learn About Labels lesson
- overhead projector, chart paper or interactive whiteboard, and appropriate markers
- sheets of red and green construction paper
- tacks, tape, etc.
- masking tape
- black markers
- small items from the teacher's desk

Recycling	
Paper Paper is made from wood pulp or trees. When it is recycled, it is broken down and mixed with water to make pulp again. Then it goes back through the paper-making process. Paper-based products include paper, newspaper, cardboard, and books.	
Glass Glass is made from sand, a naturally occurring substance. It can be melted and reformed to make other glass items.	
Metal Metal is mined from the earth. It can also be melted down and reformed again to make new things.	
Plastic Plastic is a synthetic material that is lightweight and strong and can be molded. Not all communities have the technology to recycle all types of plastic. (See Technology Resources on page 91.)	
Wood Wood can be reused in different products. Recyclers can break it down and use wood chips. Wood chips can be used for bark dust or as pulp to make paper.	
Rock Rock can be reused as gravel for roads and landscaping. Larger pieces of rock can be used for landscaping or in construction for fireplaces.	

Preparation
1. Mark off four or five areas in the classroom (four corners and a central area) using masking tape.
2. Copy the Recycling chart onto a transparency or scan into an interactive whiteboard for a class display.
3. Copy one set of Recycling Symbols for each group.
4. Make certain there are items in each group's section of the classroom that the students will likely label as "recyclable" or "non-recyclable." For example, the student papers and wood pencils are recyclable; crayons and plastic rulers are *not* easily recyclable.

Opening
1. Review what it means to recycle something. Introduce the new vocabulary word, *synthetic*. Ask if anyone knows what it means. Explain that something that is synthetic is made of manufactured materials, not materials found in nature.
2. Hold up several small items such as a ruler, an ink pen, an eraser, and scissors. Ask the students if each item is *recyclable* (can be recycled) or synthetic. Have the students explain how they know.

Part 1
1. Display the Recycling chart and read it together as a class. Discuss the materials that can be recycled. Add ideas to the overhead or whiteboard.
2. Help the students identify materials or items that cannot be recycled, such as items made of mixed materials or synthetic substances. Discuss examples of such items in the classroom (laminate countertops, student desks, pens).

Hunt for the Green *(cont.)*

Part 2

1. Give the students construction paper. Have them cut triangles from green paper and octagons from red paper.

2. Display the recycling symbol. Instruct the students to copy one recycling symbol on each green triangle.

3. On the red octagon shapes, the students will draw the recycle symbol or write the word *recycle* then draw a circle around the symbol or word and put a slash through it to indicate an item cannot be recycled.

4. Divide the students into four or five groups, corresponding to the number of previously marked off areas in the classroom. Assign each group to an area of the classroom.

5. Have the students locate and label recyclable and non-recyclable items by attaching correct labels to the items with sticky tack or tape.

Closing

1. Conduct a class discussion about ways more recyclable materials could be incorporated in a classroom (i.e., paper folders instead of plastic/vinyl, recycling bins in the room along with garbage cans, wood counter tops instead of laminate, fabric curtains instead of vinyl blinds).

2. Review the concepts of *recycle* and *synthetic* and ask how synthetic materials can be replaced with recyclable materials. Discuss why it might be important to incorporate recyclable materials in the classroom.

3. Encourage the students to remember to recycle glass, metal, and wood products, as well as paper.

Extension

Discuss with the students the materials from which other common classroom items or things the students use every day are made. Help the students realize that many things can be recycled if someone researches and finds a company that uses that material. For example, an eraser is made from rubber. If people recycle tires, could an eraser also be recycled? Why would students probably never recycle their erasers? (They use them up first.)

ELL Tip

Label items in the classroom prior to the lesson with the material from which they are made. For example, label the wood frame of a whiteboard "wood." Or label a metal paper tray "metal."

Recycling

Paper

Paper is made from wood pulp or trees. When it is recycled, it is broken down and mixed with water to make pulp again. Then it goes back through the paper-making process. Paper-based products include paper, newspaper, cardboard, and books.

Glass

Glass is made from sand, a naturally occurring substance. It can be melted and reformed to make other glass items.

Metal

Metal is mined from the earth. It can also be melted down and reformed again to make new things.

Plastic

Plastic is a synthetic material that is lightweight and strong and can be molded. Not all communities have the technology to recycle all types of plastic. (See Technology Resources on page 91.)

Wood

Wood can be reused in different products. Recyclers can break it down and use wood chips. Wood chips can be used for bark dust or as pulp to make paper.

Rock

Rocks can be reused as gravel for roads and landscaping. Larger pieces of rock can be used for landscaping or in construction for fireplaces.

Old Glass to New Product

Objective: Given a diagram and an explanation of how an item gets recycled, the students will model the process.

Vocabulary

- cullet
- facility
- furnace

Materials

- Glass Recycling Process diagram on pages 78–79
- overhead projector, chart paper or interactive whiteboard, and appropriate markers
- cardstock (eco-friendlier option: heavy scrap paper)
- recycling bin for each category of recyclables
- set of role cards for each group

Preparation

1. Copy the Glass Recycling Process diagram onto a transparency or scan it into an interactive whiteboard for class display.
2. Use cardstock to create a set of role cards for the student teams. (Each team should have 12 students.)
   - recycling bin
   - truck
   - glass
   - recycling center
   - processing facility
   - crushing machine
   - cullet
   - glass manufacturing plant
   - furnace
   - melted glass
   - glass forming machine
   - mold
3. To facilitate creation of student teams, make one set of role cards in each of two colors.

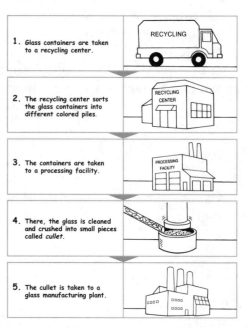

1. Glass containers are taken to a recycling center.

2. The recycling center sorts the glass containers into different colored piles.

3. The containers are taken to a processing facility.

4. There, the glass is cleaned and crushed into small pieces called *cullet*.

5. The cullet is taken to a glass manufacturing plant.

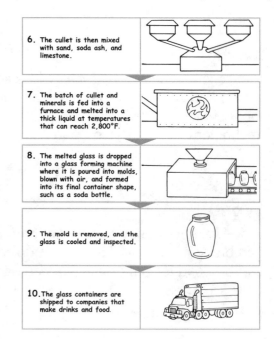

6. The cullet is then mixed with sand, soda ash, and limestone.

7. The batch of cullet and minerals is fed into a furnace and melted into a thick liquid at temperatures that can reach 2,800°F.

8. The melted glass is dropped into a glass forming machine where it is poured into molds, blown with air, and formed into its final container shape, such as a soda bottle.

9. The mold is removed, and the glass is cooled and inspected.

10. The glass containers are shipped to companies that make drinks and food.

Opening

1. Show the students the recycling bins. Ask if they have ever thought about the process of how an item gets recycled.
2. Tell the students that they will become an active part of the recycling process.

 Old Glass to New Product *(cont.)*

Part 1

1. Display the Glass Recycling Process diagram on the projector or whiteboard and discuss the steps in the recycling process.
2. Introduce and define for the students the words that describe the steps in the recycling process:

    facility— a building that makes possible some activity, such as recycling

    cullet— scraps of waste glass that can be remelted

    furnace— a large enclosed metal chamber in which fuel is burned to produce heat

Part 2

1. Review the guidelines for working together in groups. Explain that the students will work together on a team to create a human model of the recycling process.
2. Distribute one role card to each student. If there are an uneven number of students, have more than one student play the role of "cullet." Have the students form teams based on the color of their cards.
3. Remind the students to refer to the Glass Recycling Process diagram posted in the room.
4. Allow the students time to prepare, review the recycling process, and practice their demonstration.
5. Direct the teams to present their model to the class.

Closing

1. Divide students into smaller groups to evaluate and discuss the recycling process. Ask the students to answer the following questions in their groups.
   - What did you learn about the recycling process?
   - In what ways is the process effective?
   - What ideas do you have for improving the process?
2. As time allows, have group members share their responses with the class. Ask the students how they can apply their learning to their lives. (I know now that many types of glass can be recycled, and I will try to remember to recycle glass.)

Extension

Have the students use technology or other resources to research and learn about a different recycling process, such as paper or metal. The students may diagram the process they researched and post it as part of a class bulletin board display.

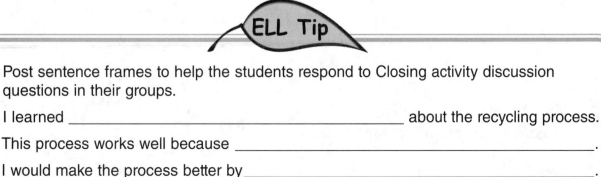

ELL Tip

Post sentence frames to help the students respond to Closing activity discussion questions in their groups.

I learned _____ about the recycling process.

This process works well because _____.

I would make the process better by_____.

Glass Recycling Process

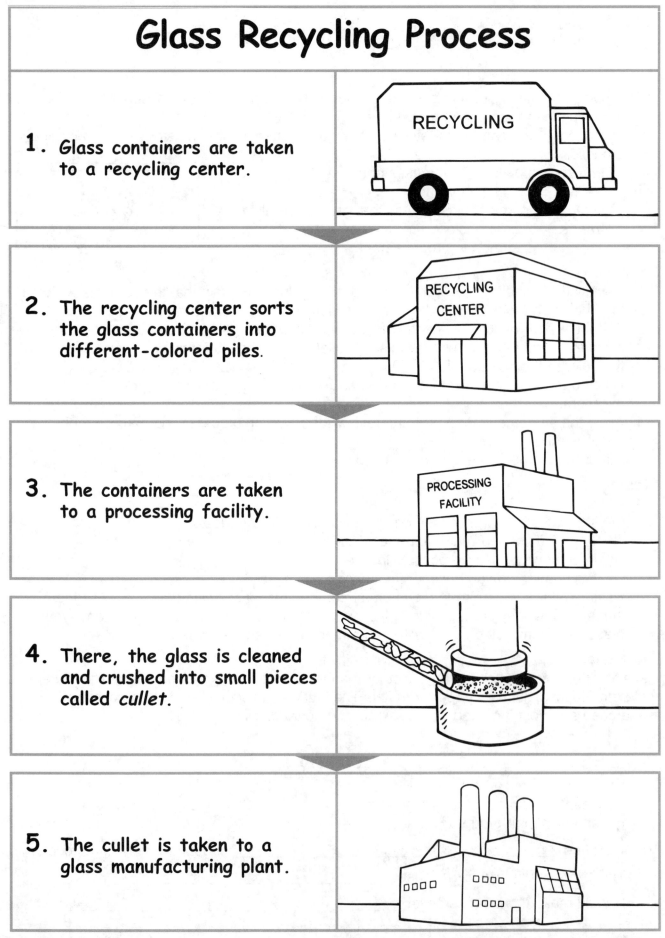

1. Glass containers are taken to a recycling center.

2. The recycling center sorts the glass containers into different-colored piles.

3. The containers are taken to a processing facility.

4. There, the glass is cleaned and crushed into small pieces called *cullet*.

5. The cullet is taken to a glass manufacturing plant.

Glass Recycling Process *(cont.)*

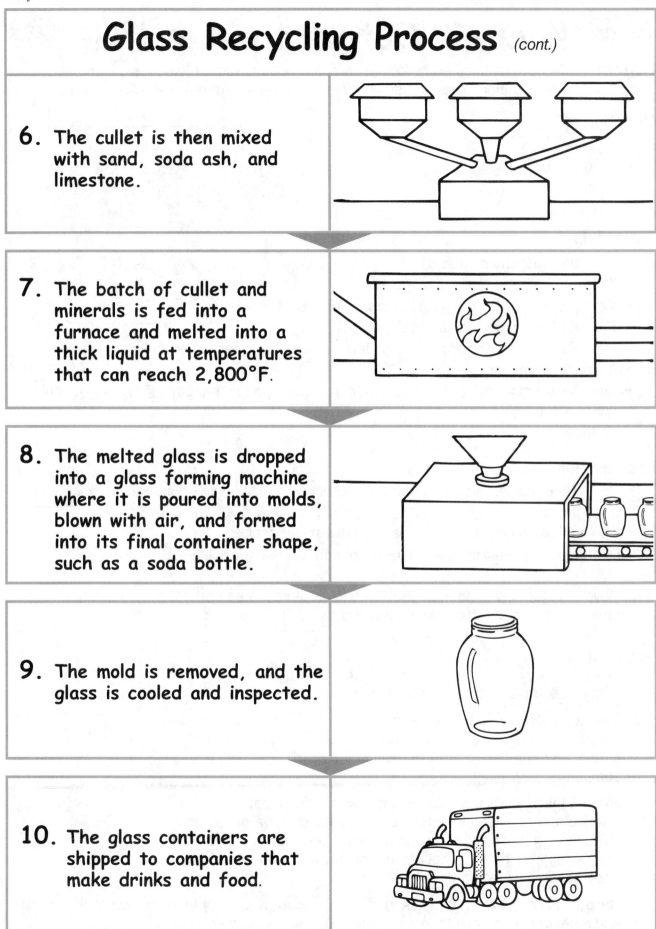

6. The cullet is then mixed with sand, soda ash, and limestone.

7. The batch of cullet and minerals is fed into a furnace and melted into a thick liquid at temperatures that can reach 2,800°F.

8. The melted glass is dropped into a glass forming machine where it is poured into molds, blown with air, and formed into its final container shape, such as a soda bottle.

9. The mold is removed, and the glass is cooled and inspected.

10. The glass containers are shipped to companies that make drinks and food.

Keep It Out of the Landfill

Objective: Given pictures and information about ways to recycle electronic items, the students will analyze electronic devices and determine an appropriate recycling option.

Vocabulary

- E-waste
- Tech Trash
- electronic
- technology

Materials

- E-waste Cartoon on page 82
- Types of E-Waste cards on page 83
- Where Does My E-Waste Go? cards on pages 84
- E-waste Destinations chart on page 85
- overhead projector or interactive whiteboard and appropriate markers
- 2 sheets of cardstock
- advertisements/brochures about local community groups that participate in electronic waste recycling
- scissors

Preparation

1. Copy the E-waste Cartoon onto a transparency or scan it into an interactive whiteboard.
2. Copy the two sets of cards onto cardstock. Cut apart the cards to use for the whole-class activity in Part 2. Make extra sets as needed.
3. Read E-waste Destinations to familiarize yourself with possible recycling options for electronic waste.
4. Have the students bring in advertisements and brochures from local community organizations that participate in recycling.

Opening

1. Write the following phrases on the board: *E-waste* and *Tech Trash*. Ask the students what they think these phrases mean.

2. Tell the students the "E" stands for electronic. *Electronic* devices have transistors or silicon chips that control an electric current. Examples of electronic devices include TVs, radios, and computers.

3. Explain that *Tech* is short for technology, or things that use science and engineering to help us do things or solve problems. Even though these items—computers, cell phones, calculators— are useful, they break or get old and often we throw them away. They become waste or trash.

4. Have each student turn and talk to a partner about what they think the words *electronic* and *technology* mean. Call on a few students to share their ideas.

Keep It Out of the Landfill *(cont.)*

Part 1

1. Display the E-Waste Cartoon. Allow time for the students to view the cartoon.

2. Tell the students that the computer does not want to go to the landfill, and the class will need to help it find another place to go.

3. Ask the students to suggest places where an old computer might go. Assist the students with the following suggestions as necessary. (An old computer can go back to the store, back to the manufacturer, or be donated to a school or a job-training facility.)

Part 2

1. Display the two sets of cards for the class. Match the Types of E-Waste cards to the appropriate Where Does My E-Waste Go? cards. If desired, distribute student copies and have the students complete the matching activity on their own.

2. Have the students work together as a class to find pictures depicting local stores and other organizations who accept electronic items for recycling.

3. Display the pictures on a bulletin board or poster.

4. Have the students add the cards under or near the proper location (i.e., monitor—charitable organization). Consider making this an ongoing activity.

Part 3

1. Have each student create a list indicating which items each organization takes back for recycling.

2. Direct the students to take the list home, or e-mail the list to their parents, to share recycling suggestions with family members.

cell phone

recycling organization

Closing

1. Review the terms *E-waste*, *Tech Trash*, *electronic*, and *technology*.

2. Reinforce the students' understanding of electronic technology—and those things which become E-waste—by inviting them to write a riddle about an electronic device.

Extension

Check with administrators about the possibility of conducting an E-waste drive. Have the students collect used electronic items. They could use any money generated for specific school projects.

ELL Tip

Provide pictures for each electronic device listed in the matching activity in Part 2 to aid the students with learning the new vocabulary.

Keep It Out of the Landfill (cont.)

E-Waste Cartoon

Keep It Out of the Landfill (cont.)

Types of E-Waste

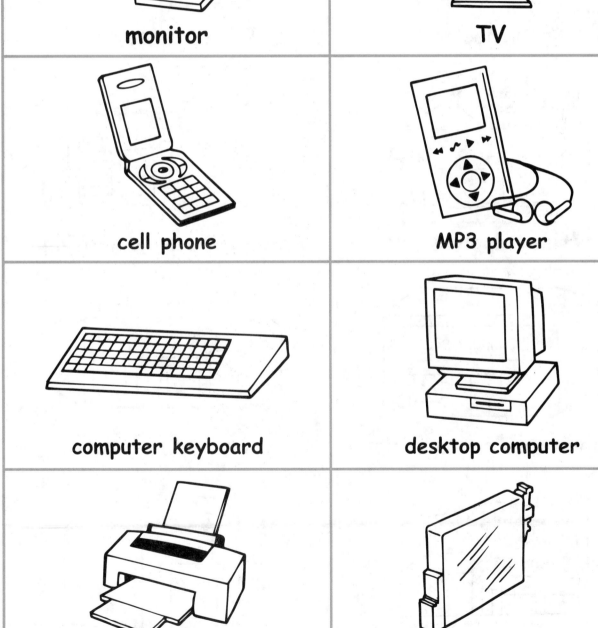

monitor	TV
cell phone	MP3 player
computer keyboard	desktop computer
printer	ink cartridge

Keep It Out of the Landfill *(cont.)*

Where Does My E-Waste Go?

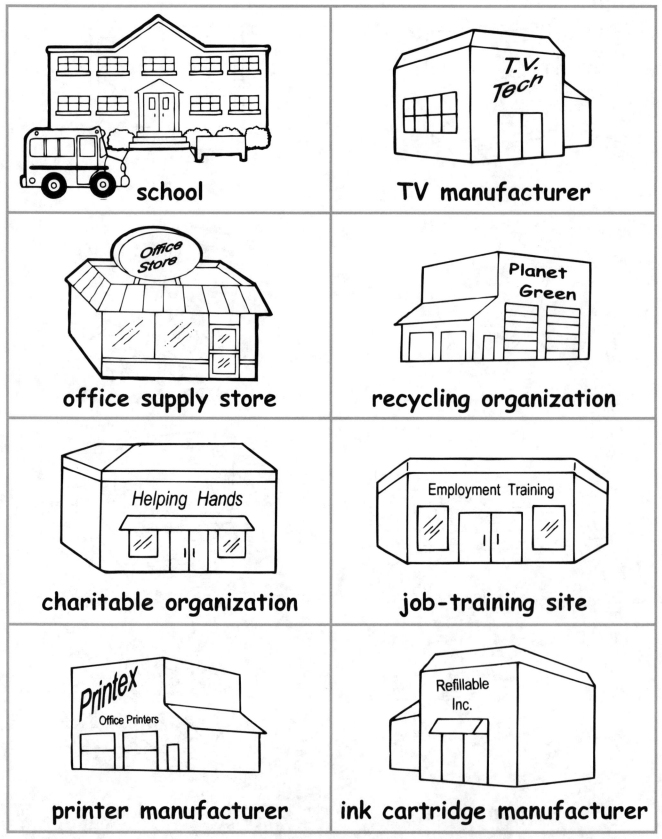

school

TV manufacturer

office supply store

recycling organization

charitable organization

job-training site

printer manufacturer

ink cartridge manufacturer

Keep It Out of the Landfill (cont.)

E-Waste Destinations

Desktop and Laptop computers
- local public and private schools
- some computer manufacturers
- charitable organizations
- job-training sites

TVs
- manufacturers—check with individual companies

Cell phones
- office supply stores
- charitable organizations
- cell phone companies

Monitors
- local public and private schools
- charitable organizations
- some office supply stores

MP3 players
- recycling organizations

Game consoles
- recycling organizations

Ink cartridges and printers
- charitable organizations
- office supply stores
- manufacturers—check with individual companies

Digital cameras
- recycling organizations

Rechargeable batteries
- office supply stores

Scanners, hard drives, keyboards, mice, speakers, cords, and cables
- charitable organizations

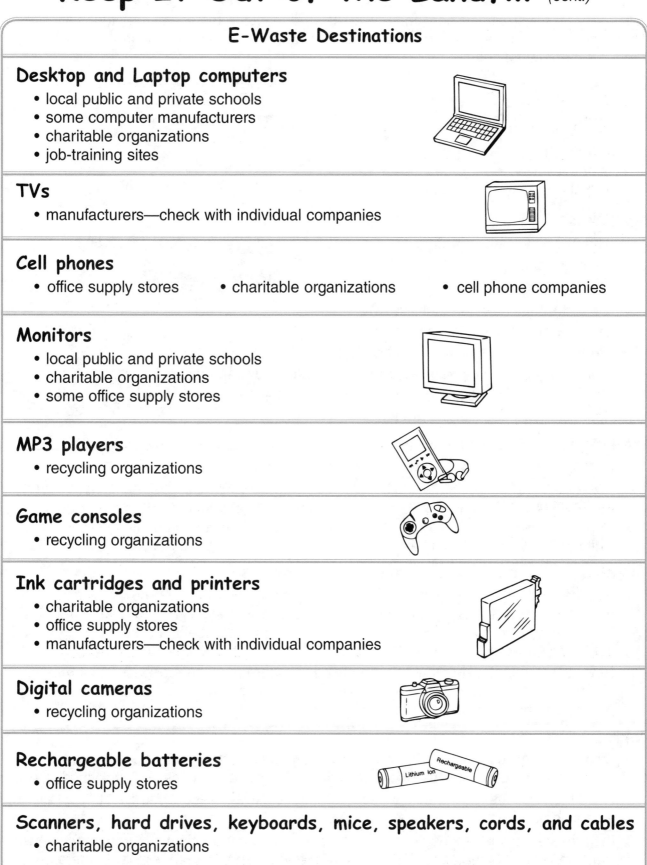

The Greenhouse Effect

Objective: Given an explanation, definitions, and resource materials, the students will draw a diagram to explain the greenhouse effect on our atmosphere and demonstrate this effect through experimentation.

Vocabulary

- greenhouse effect
- greenhouse gas
- ozone
- ozone layer
- global warming

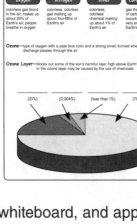

Materials

- The Air We Breathe on page 88
- lamp (for each group)
- shoebox (for each group)
- small thermometer (for each group)
- overhead projector, chart paper or interactive whiteboard, and appropriate markers
- student dictionaries, encyclopedias, or other reference materials
- clear or light-colored plastic (eco-friendlier option: discarded plastic wrap)
- darker piece of plastic (eco-friendlier option: discarded pieces of garbage or leaf bags)
- Technology Resources on page 92.

Preparation

1. Gather reference books and other resources for student use.
2. If you have access to the Internet, compile links for appropriate sites (as suggested on the Technology Resources page) into a document for student access.
3. Copy the The Air We Breathe onto a transparency or scan it into an interactive whiteboard. White out or hide the definitions for each vocabulary term.

Opening

1. Ask the students if they have ever seen a greenhouse. Ask if they know how a greenhouse works. (The glass panels on the greenhouse let light and heat in from the sun. The glass keeps the heat from escaping. The inside heats up, like the inside of a car heats up when it is parked in the sun.)
2. Review with the students the definition of *atmosphere* (a mixture of gases that make up the air that surrounds our planet). Explain that tiny particles, such as dust, water, and pollen, also float around in the atmosphere.

Part 1

1. Display the vocabulary terms from The Air We Breathe on the overhead or whiteboard. Encourage the students to use dictionaries and other reference books to define these terms.
2. Have the students form groups to research further the concept of Earth's atmosphere and its elements.
3. Instruct the student groups to use their information to create simple pie graphs to show the composition of the atmosphere (or use the chart on page 88), similar to the one shown on page 87.

The Greenhouse Effect *(cont.)*

Part 1 *(cont.)*

Atmosphere

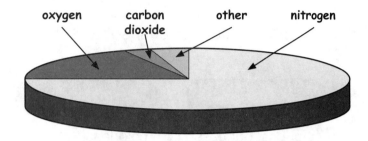

oxygen   carbon dioxide   other   nitrogen

Part 2

1. Have the students use approved reference materials to research and learn about how *greenhouse gases* work to create the *greenhouse effect and global warming*.

2. Ask the students to draw diagrams showing how greenhouse gases affect the atmosphere. (If necessary, assist students with this task.)

3. Call on two or three student volunteers to explain their diagrams to the class.

Part 3

1. Have each group of students (from Part 1) use a light-colored piece of plastic, a darker piece of plastic, a box, and a lamp to create a model of the greenhouse effect.

   • The box represents Earth.

   • The light piece of plastic represents the natural atmosphere.

   • The lamp serves as the sun.

2. Have the students set up group demonstrations to show how our atmosphere holds in some heat.

3. Place the thermometer in the box, cover it with the light-colored plastic, and record the temperature.

4. Next have the students add the layer of darker plastic over the box. Tell the class this represents carbon dioxide emissions and other greenhouse gases.

5. Have each group record the change in temperature.

Closing

Discuss with the students how greenhouse gases affect Earth's temperature and the implications that has for people, animals, and plants.

Extension

Write the vocabulary words on the board. Divide the students into two or more teams. Have each team work together to write sentences using the vocabulary words correctly—one sentence for each word. The first team to use all the vocabulary words wins.

ELL Tip

Work with a small group to complete the graphic organizer, The Air We Breathe.

Look up the terms in a reference book, and assist the students in rewording the definitions in simple terms they can understand.

The Air We Breathe

Atmosphere—the mixture of gases that surrounds a planet; air

oxygen	nitrogen	other	carbon dioxide
colorless gas found in the air; makes up about 20% of Earth's air; people breathe in oxygen	colorless, odorless gas making up about four-fifths of Earth's air	colorless, odorless chemicals making up about 1% of Earth's air	gas that is a mixture of carbon and oxygen; occurs naturally in very small amounts of Earth's air; plants absorb carbon dioxide

Ozone—type of oxygen with a pale blue color and a strong smell; formed when an electrical discharge passes through the air

Ozone Layer—blocks out some of the sun's harmful rays; high above Earth's surface; hole in the ozone layer may be caused by the use of chemicals

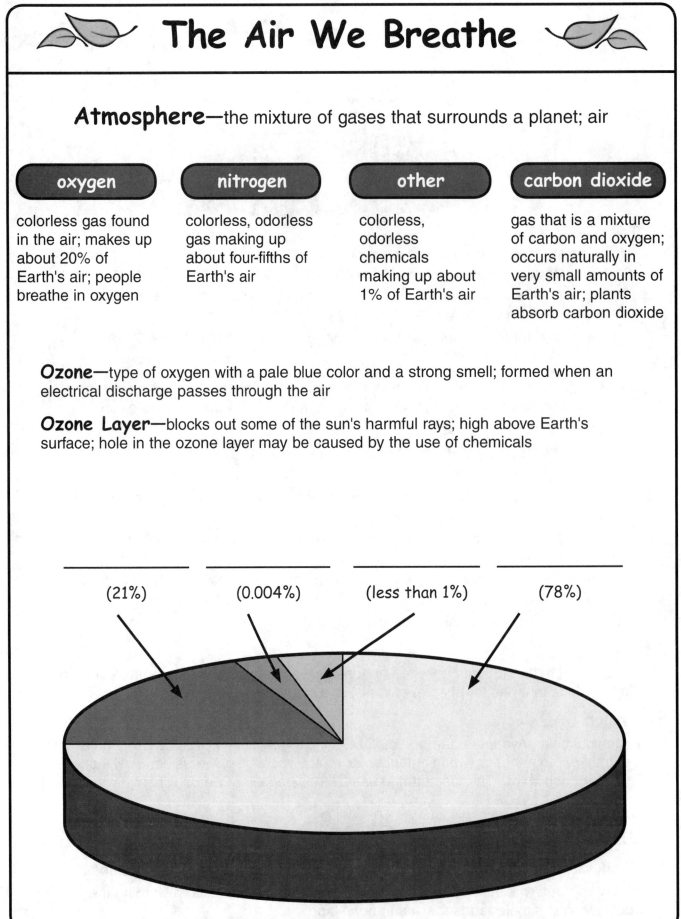

(21%)   (0.004%)   (less than 1%)   (78%)

 # Living Green

Objective: Given the opportunity to consider what people might do to "Live Green," the students will write questions and interview a family member. **Note:** This lesson will take two days of class time.

Materials

- Becoming G-R-R-R-R-R-EEN—Learning the Rs on pages 20–21
- overhead projector, chart paper or interactive whiteboard, and appropriate markers
- piece of paper for each student (eco-friendlier option: individual whiteboard and appropriate marker)
- sheet of writing paper for each student
- poster board

Preparation

1. Write the following sentence frames on a transparency or interactive whiteboard:

> One thing I do to help the environment is _____ .
>
> I save electricity by _____ .
>
> I reduce garbage by _____ .
>
> I recycle _____ .
>
> I reuse _____ and use it for _____ .

Opening

1. Have the students come up one at a time to complete a sentence frame.
2. Have the rest of the class follow along by writing their responses on pieces of paper, individual whiteboards, or participating with an interactive whiteboard.

Part 1

1. Review the definitions and concepts of *Going Green* and *environmentally friendly* (See the Environmental Perspectives unit on page 12).
2. Ask the students to consider what they would like to know about things other people do to help the environment.
3. Have each student write several questions (three or more) to ask a family member or family friend about "Living Green" or performing environmentally friendly actions.

Living Green *(cont.)*

Part 2

1. Direct the students to take their questions home to ask a family member or friend.

2. Remind the students to bring their interview questions and responses back to class the following day.

3. The following day, review the concept of Living Green as students share their interview results.

4. Work together as a class to create a poster entitled "Living Green." Incorporate responses from the student interviews.

Closing

1. Begin by briefly reviewing with the students the meaning of each R word. (See Becoming G-R-R-R-R-R-EEN—Learn the Rs.)

2. Hold a class discussion, focusing on the following questions:

   • How can you respond at home to be more environmentally friendly? At school? In the community?

   • What is one goal that you could make for how you will respond to living Green in the future?

3. Have each student write a journal entry describing one new thing they learned about making choices that are good for the environment from their interview experiences.

4. Invite student volunteers to share their journal entries with the class.

5. If time allows, encourage student volunteers to elaborate on experiences they have had at home and in the community relating to the R words.

ELL Tip

Have the students practice asking questions with partners before writing their interview questions on paper. A family member may help the student record responses as necessary. If the student cannot interview a family member, have him or her interview a classroom aide or another person at school.

 # Technology Resources

Think Green

Greenovation
Dedicated to the greening of America's schools through education
http://www.greenovation.com

Learn About Labels
Post-consumer waste sample label
http://www.ecosmarte.com/images/Post%20 Consumer%20Waste%20Logo.jpg

Recycling Logos Explained
http://www.barefootpress.com/blog/?tag=recycled-logo

Heal the Planet
Introduction to Ecology
http://kids.nceas.ucsb.edu/ecology/ecoindex.html

Energy Efficiency
How much energy things use
http://michaelbluejay.com/electricity/howmuch.html

Reduce

Sample Paperless Classroom
http://www.abpc21.org/withoutpaper.html

Reuse

Precious Rainwater
University of Wisconsin Extension Environmental Resource Center
http://www.uwex.edu/erc/youth.html

The Weather Channel
Local weather and rainfall information
http://www.weather.com/

EPA WaterSense Kids—A Day in the Life of a Drop
http://www.epa.gov/WaterSense/kids/index.htm

Refuse

Avoid Plastic
General information about plastic
http://pslc.ws/paul.html

Recycle

Recycled Materials Recovery Center
List of plastic types and recycle symbols
http://www.epa.gov/recyclecity/print/recovery.htm

Hunt for the Green
FTC consumer alerts for labeling
http://www.ftc.gov/bcp/edu/pubs/consumer/alerts/ alt049.shtm

http://www.ftc.gov/bcp/edu/pubs/consumer/general/ gen02.shtm

Find Out What Your Community Accepts for Recycling
http://www.earth911.com

Keep It Out of the Landfill
Environmental Protection Agency
http://www.epa.gov/recyclecity/print/supermarket.htm

Plastic Recycling Information
http://environment.about.com/od/earthtalkcolumns/a/ recycleplastics.htm

Environmentally Friendly Gift Cards
http://www.earthworkssystem.com/index.html

Collective Good
Mobile phone recycling
http://www.collectivegood.com/

Cristina Foundation
http://www.cristina.org/

Computers for Schools
http://www.pcrr.com/pcsforschools.asp

Goodwill
http://www.goodwill.org

Technology Resources *(cont.)*

Recycle *(cont.)*

Cardboard
http://www.corrugated.org/Recycling/
RecyclingProcess.aspx

Paper
*http://www.tappi.org/paperu/all_about_paper/earth_*
answers/EarthAnswers_Recycle.pdf

http://www.gp.com/EducationalinNature/paper/
recycling.html

Glass
http://www.reachoutmichigan.org/funexperiments/
agesubject/lessons/newton/GlssRecycl.html

http://www.wisegeek.com/how-are-glass-bottles-
recycled.htm

http://earth911.com/blog/2009/05/04/minn-fifth-grader-
turns-old-glass-into-booming-business/

Research

The Greenhouse Effect
Environmental Protection Agency Kids Site
http://www.epa.gov/climatechange/kids/greenhouse.html

EPA Planet Protectors Club (Hidden Reasons to Reduce, Reuse, Recycle)
http://www.epa.gov/waste/education/pdfs/k00-001.pdf

University of California–San Diego
http://earthguide.ucsd.edu/earthguide/diagrams/
greenhouse/

Enchanted Learning
http://www.enchantedlearning.com/subjects/
astronomy/planets/earth/Greenhouse.html

University Corporation for Atmospheric Research
http://eo.ucar.edu/kids/green/warming4.htm

Teacher Reference
http://www.ucar.edu/learn/1_3_1.htm

Additional Resources

Lessons About Recycling
http://www.mde.state.md.us/Programs/LandPrograms/
Recycling/Education/process.asp

EPA Planet Protectors Club
www.epa.gov/waste/education/kids/

Curriculum Activities (K–5)
http://www.epa.gov/epawaste/education/teach_curric.
htm#kids

Online Games
United States Environmental
Protection Agency
http://www.epa.gov/kids/

National Geographic
http://kids.nationalgeographic.com/Games/

Environmentally Friendly School Supplies
http://slowburnproductions.wordpress.
com/2006/09/18/environmentally-friendly-pencil-lust/

http://www.amazon.com/gp/product/
B000UZVLXK?ie=UTF8&s=office-
products&qid=1186019536&sr=8-1

National Institute of Environmental Health Sciences (NIEHS)
Ways to eliminate waste and protect
the environment
http://www.kids.niehs.nih.gov/recycle.htm

Glossary

atmosphere	the mixture of gases that surrounds a planet; air
biodegradable	something that can be broken down naturally by bacteria
bulk	(to buy in) large quantities; not in individual packages
carbon dioxide	a gas that is a mixture of carbon and oxygen
carbon footprint	the amount of carbon dioxide that enters the atmosphere during daily activities
chemicals	substances that interact with each other
closing the loop	using an item again, instead of it going into a landfill
conserve	to save something from loss or waste
consume	to use up an item
consumer	someone that uses a product or service
crude oil	oil in its natural state before it is processed
cullet	scraps of waste glass that can be remelted
cycle	a series of steps that is done over and over again
decompose	to rot or decay
disposable	made to be thrown away after use
durable	strong enough to be reused

 # Glossary *(cont.)*

electronic	a device powered by tiny amounts of electricity produced by electrons
emission	a substance going into the air
environment	natural world of land, sea, air, including plants and animals
environmentally friendly	something that is good for the environment
E-waste	electronic waste
excessive	too much
facility	a building that makes possible some activity, such as recycling
fiber	a long, thin thread of material such as cotton, wool, hemp, or nylon; includes wood fibers
fossil fuel	Fuel is something that burns, like coal, oil, or gas. A fossil fuel is formed from the remains of fossils, or prehistoric plants and animals.
furnace	a large enclosed metal chamber in which fuel is burned to produce heat
global warming	combined result of human-caused emissions of greenhouse gases and the increase in Earth's atmospheric and oceanic temperatures
Green	describes something that is good for the environment
greenhouse effect	effect of water and carbon dioxide absorbing outgoing infrared radiation, raising Earth's temperature
greenhouse gas	any of the atmospheric gases that contribute to the greenhouse effect
hazardous	dangerous
kilowatt hour	1,000 watts of energy used for one hour

 # Glossary *(cont.)*

landfill	garbage that is stacked and covered with earth
natural gas	a gas that is found beneath the earth's surface
nonrenewable	a resource that can be used up
ozone	form of oxygen that is formed when an electrical discharge passes through the air
ozone layer	A layer high above Earth's surface that blocks out some of the sun's harmful rays
packaging	the wrapping, box, or container in which an item is sold
perspective	the way people look at things; how they view a particular situation or the world
petroleum	a thick, oily liquid found below the earth's surface
plastic	a light, strong, synthetic substance that can be molded into different shapes and thicknesses
pollution	environmental contamination with man-made waste
post-consumer waste	materials people have already used and thrown away
pre-consumer material	waste from the manufacturing process, before people have used the product
process	an organized series of steps or actions that produce a particular result
rechargeable	an electrical item (battery) that can be charged and used again
recycle	processing old items to make new products; when something goes through a process again
recyclable	item that can be recycled

 # Glossary *(cont.)*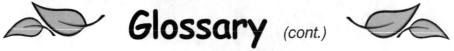

reduce	to lessen in any way, such as to lower the amount; make something smaller; use less
refillable	able to be refilled and used again
refuse	to say you will not do something or accept something; to make a choice not to do something;
repurpose	to use something again in a new way
research	to study and find out more about a topic
respond	to reply, give an answer, or to react to something
reusable	something that can be used again
reuse	to use something again
source	the place, person, or thing from which something comes
STOP	<u>S</u>top, <u>T</u>hink, <u>O</u>ptions, <u>P</u>articipate
synthetic	made of manufactured materials, not materials found in nature
Tech Trash	technology trash, including old computers, cell phones, etc.
technology	things that use science and engineering to help us do things or solve problems
waste	n. something left over not used or discarded v. comsume or spend in a useless manner
watt	a unit of measurement used to measure electricity